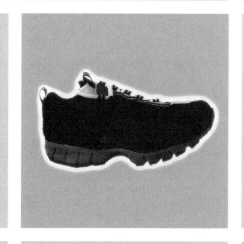

The Bazaar Books Series

The Bazaar Books Series aims to explore the basic labor and economic issues behind everyday products and commodities. Written and edited by experienced journalists, each book is jammed full of facts, figures, cartoons, and commentary from a wide range of sources, and delves into the cultural and social history of the product in question.

The Sneaker Book

Anatomy of an Industry and an Icon

TOM VANDERBILT

The New Press New York

From *The Bonfire of the Vanities*, by Tom Wolfe.
Copyright (c) 1988 by Tom Wolfe.
Reprinted by permission of Farrar, Straus
& Giroux, Inc.

From "An Interview with Run-D.M.C.,"
in *Grand Royal #3*, 1996.
Reprinted by permission of Daniel A. Field.

From "Domination by Design," by Randy Gragg
in *Metropolis*, June 1997.
Reprinted by permission. Copyright (c) 1997
Bellerophon Publications, Inc.

From "The Tyranny of the Swoosh,"
in *AIGA Journal of Graphic Design*.
Reprinted by permission of Phil Patton.

From "The Coolhunt," by Malcolm Gladwell,
in *The New Yorker*.
Reprinted by permission of author.

From "The Nike Psyche," by Josh Feit, in *Willamette
Week*, Portland, Oregon, August 28, 1997.
Reprinted by permission from *Willamette Week*.

From "Fast on His Feet: An Interview with
Gordon Thompson III," in *Purple Prose #12*, 1997.
Reprinted by permission of Ellein Fleiss.

From "It's Gotta Be Da Shoes" by R. Barff &
J. Austen, in *Environment and Planning A*, 1993.
Volume 25, pages 1103–1114.
Reprinted by permission of Pion Limited, London.

From *Just Do It*, by Donald Katz.
Copyright (c) 1994 by Donald Katz.
Reprinted by permission of Random House, Inc.

From "The Globetrotting Sneaker," by Cynthia Enloe
in *Ms.* magazine, March/April 1995.
Reprinted by permission of *Ms.* magazine, (c) 1995.

From *The Sponsored Life*, by Leslie Savan.
Reprinted by permission of author.

From *Where the Suckers Moon*, by Randall
Rothenberg. Copyright (c) Randall Rothenberg.
Reprinted by permission of Alfred A. Knopf, Inc.

From *Washingtoon*, by Mark Alan Stamaty.
Reprinted by permission of Mark Alan Stamaty.

From *Doonesbury*, by Garry Trudeau.
© 1997 G.B. Trudeau. Reprinted with permission of
UNIVERSAL PRESS SYNDICATE. All rights reserved.

From "The Sound of Summer Running"
in *Dandelion Wine* by Ray Bradbury.
Reprinted by permission of Don Congdon
Associates, Inc.
Copyright (c) 1956 by the Curtis Publishing Co.,
renewed 1984 by Ray Bradbury.

From *The White Boy Shuffle*, by Paul Beatty.
Copyright (c) 1996 by Paul Beatty.
Reprinted by permission of Houghton Mifflin
Company. All rights reserved.

From *The Best Seat in the House*, by Spike Lee.
Copyright (c) 1997 by Spike Lee.
Reprinted by permission of Crown Publishers Inc.

From "Sneakers," by Alisa Solomon, in *Venue:
An International Literary Magazine*, Fall 1997.
Reprinted by permission of author.

Published in the United States by The New Press, New York
Distributed by W.W. Norton & Company, Inc., New York

The New Press was established in 1990 as a not-for-profit alternative to the large,
commercial publishing houses currently dominating the book publishing industry.
The New Press operates in the public interest rather than for private gain,
and is committed to publishing, in innovative ways, works of educational, cultural,
and community value that might not be deemed sufficiently profitable.

Book design by Smyth and Whiteside (BAD)

Printed in the United States of America   9 8 7 6 5 4 3 2

Contents

We are grateful for permission to use the following images:

Page 10: Converse advertisement, courtesy of Converse
Page 35: photograph of Run-D.M.C. © Ricky Powell
Page 106: photograph of workers © Tim Jewett/The Oregonian
Page 150: photograph of Niketown, New York, courtesy of Nike

Sneaker photographs on the following pages were provided courtesy:

Airwalk: 12, 16, 32, 58, 78, 90, 94, 110, 118, 140, 158, 162
ASICS®: 18, 22, 30, 34, 50, 64, 80, 84, 92, 96, 120, 124, 136, 142, 152
Converse Inc.: 8, 10, 36, 112, 128, 150
Etonic Worldwide: 28, 40, 56, 108, 132, 160
Keds/Striderite: 46, 86, 130
New Balance: 2, 14, 66, 76, 88, 122, 134, 148, 156
Nike Inc.: 6, 44, 60, 70, 98, 100, 116
Puma: 20, 38, 42, 52, 54, 62, 72, 104, 106, 126, 144, 154
Reebok: 4, 26, 68, 102, 146
Vans, Inc.: 24, 82
Checkerboard shoe design is a registered trademark of Vans.

Figures

Preface

SOMETIME JUST BEFORE THE CLOSE of the 1970s I joined one
of two pioneering consumer movements born of that decade:
computers and sneakers. My PC induction came late and on the cusp
of obsolescence: a slate-gray Commodore 64 (with a tape deck
for memory, no less), purchased several years later. But I was more
or less at the vanguard of the other movement. On an otherwise
unremarkable summer weekend in the suburban Midwest, my
parents accompanied me to the local shopping mall, to a novel
and exciting store where the employees dressed like referees. It was
there that I bought the shoes. They were, I recall in fuzzy retrospect,
a pair of Nike Cortez, blue with a white stripe on the side (called
a "swoosh," as a label on the tongue explained) and nestled snugly
in a crisp orange cardboard box. Suddenly, a decade of personal
footwear history, checkered with pedestrian oxfords and threadbare
canvas sneakers that I can hardly remember now, vanished before my
eyes. Nothing I would later buy for my feet would ever recreate the
sublime feel and psychic rush I experienced when I slipped into the
brilliantine nylon and resilient foam and bounded out of the store.

Little did I anticipate then that Nike—still officially listed in
financial documents as Blue Ribbon Sports—would go on to become

one of the world's most recognized brands, or that the shoes I was wearing would soon adorn a majority of American feet, or that in ten years the newspapers would be full of stories about kids my age killing each other for the shoes I so desired. The signs, however, were clear. The mere fact that I should have felt myself so transformed by the purchase of a pair of "gym shoes" (as they were called in the Midwest), when none previous had registered on my consciousness, was a harbinger of a new feeling sweeping the country: sneakers were no longer simply sneakers. Something else was at work, an inexorable pull that had me explaining to my parents why they should spend three times the normal amount on their child's sneakers, which were already preciously being referred to as "athletic shoes."

My fascination held fast through succeeding pairs of Adidas Sambas and Stan Smiths, Converse Jack Purcells, Nike Air Flights, and countless other sneakers. Even if I no longer carefully duplicated sneaker company logos on my school books nor embossed the soles and sides with my own penmanship, there was still a giddiness as I opened each box and carefully laced the shoe, luxuriating in the new, slightly chemical smell as one does with a car. For the most part, however, my interest in the product stopped at the product itself. Like most consumers, I never stopped to consider where these shoes had come from, who had made them, how much profit each company was pulling in because of my purchase, or even how much they had spent to make me aware of what they were selling. And while I was aware of the cultural potency of sneaker advertising, whether it was Spike Lee playing gadfly to Michael Jordan or James Dean lounging about in Jack Purcells (yes, he wore khakis too), I never stopped to question why a shoe that had been a whimsical, if quotidian, emblem of childhood now assumed such prominence in the national consciousness.

One of the apparent paradoxes of the so-called post-industrial era is that while service and information is taken to be the dominant currency, the number of manufactured products continues to multiply. Sneakers, sunglasses, soda pop—you will find many more brands of these products now than you ever would have in the days of the "industrial economy." And under the logic of the brand extension, it seems as if any company can make just about any product. Sneaker maker Nike produces athletic-oriented sunglasses, so it should have come as no surprise that Oakley, a maker of expensive sunglasses, announced in the fall of 1997 that it was gearing up to issue its first line of athletic shoes (the company began as a motorcycle-parts supplier). Yet despite the retail bounty, we know less and less about what actually goes into putting such things on store shelves. The efforts of various activists to expose the sweatshop conditions under which clothes and other products are made here and abroad has raised the awareness of many consumers. It is difficult, however, to counter the bevy of glamorous images in which a product is draped. Even a "Made in the U.S.A." tag reveals little, since many of the product's components may have been manufactured somewhere else, only to be assembled here.

This book grows out of my own interest in the sneaker as product and as cultural phenomenon. It is a decidedly ambivalent relationship. On the one hand, I share the fetishistic enthusiasm for sneakers common to so many American consumers. Yet behind the populist veneer lies a number of questions, some of them uncomfortable.

Where does my money go when I purchase a pair of sneakers? How much is simply channeled back into crafting fantastical commercials or paying an already wealthy celebrity–athlete to endow the shoe with proper aura? How is what I'm buying produced, and who is producing it? Despite—or perhaps because of—the sneaker's popularity, it is often difficult to find much historical context for the shoe's ascendance, or to examine what its popularity might suggest about America. Where did the sneaker come from, both in a literal and historical sense? Who are the companies behind the logos? Who's buying all of those sneakers and how much are they spending? Why is Nike heralded by economists and lampooned by *Doonesbury*?

    I want to cut through the symbolism and hype, sever my own nostalgic and material ties, and get at the thing itself, which, if it were disassembled into its raw materials, would be worth pennies. The makers of new, higher-end sneakers tend to emphasize the soles, showing you what they've got—usually some viscous fluid or system of synthetic rubber cylinders—through plastic windows. If only the sneaker companies themselves were open to the same scrutiny.

This is not meant to be a book about Nike, but continual reference to that company is unavoidable in a book about the athletic shoe industry, since Nike controls nearly half the retail sneaker market, wielding inordinate influence and driving much of the industry's direction. (See Figure 1) One indication of Nike's power is belied by the decision of several competitors, including Fila and Adidas, to open offices in relatively far-flung Portland, presumably to be closer to Nike head-quarters and perhaps to lure a designer or two away. If this book had

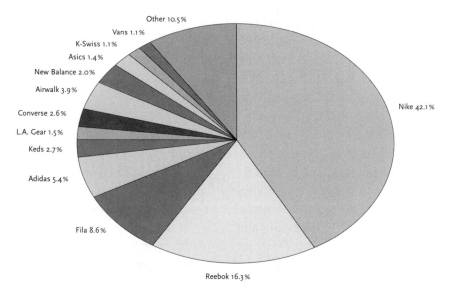

FIGURE 1 *U.S. Athletic Footwear Market Share*, 1996 (est.)

been written in the 1960s, Converse would take center stage; in the 1970s, Adidas. In the next decade another company may very well displace Nike from its roost, but in the 1990s it has been Nike that changed the very meaning of what an athletic shoe company represents, in terms of reach, sales, profit margins, and cultural impact. One marketing company even found Nike to have the highest logo recognition among children it had ever recorded.

Another caveat concerns terminology. While Nike and Reebok would prefer that their products be referred to by their "proper" name (that is, running shoe, tennis shoe, cross-trainer) or more generally by "athletic shoe," the simple fact is that most people do not wear such shoes for athletics. Also, "sneaker" has endured in the vernacular as a catchall term, which may hint that the consumer has been slow to accept the myriad marketing pitches calling it otherwise. Technically speaking, "sneakers" are simple shoes with stitched canvas uppers and vulcanized rubber soles—the kind sold by Keds, Converse, and other companies, including a shot of new fashion-oriented firms. The "athletic shoe" contains hardly any actual rubber, instead using polyurethane foam and EVA for its soles and nylon, leather, or a specially trademarked hybrid synthetic fabric for its upper. The industry first generally lumped the shoes together in its accounting, but has gradually adopted different categories for each type of shoe, rubrics such as "athleisure" or "athletic casual." Further complicating this is the system of classification used by the Census Bureau and others in tabulating imports and industry figures. "Nonrubber footwear," for example, includes both leather basketball shoes and stiletto pumps from Italy; "rubber footwear," meanwhile, can include both hip waders and sneakers. The following description of the market from the 1994 U.S. Industrial Outlook report is tellingly complex: "Consumption of athletic footwear, including imports and domestic production of rubber-fabric 'sneakers,' reached a high of about 565 million pairs in 1992 but declined about one percent in 1993. Athletic footwear represented about 38 percent of combined nonrubber and rubber-fabric footwear consumption of about 1.5 billion pairs in 1993." An additional problem in tracing the history of sneaker sales is that there are few reliable indicators for gauging the size of the sneaker market before the 1960s.

Americans now buy over 350 million pairs of sneakers a year. In the 1950s, they purchased less than 40 million pairs. What changed in the intervening years? Sneakers went—seemingly overnight—from childhood summer staples to serious athletic instruments, but the transition is hazy. Historians have tracked the inspirations behind various fashion movements, but within that milieu the sneaker lies low in the order of things, an object of polite condescension. Sneakers are simply something people wear, one might reason. What more to it could there possibly be? The sneaker is emblematic of many products today: we expend much energy dreaming about and acquiring objects, but comparatively little reflecting about where they came from, what might have gone into their manufacture, how and why their design is different today than it was ten years ago, why we may have desired them, and why they even exist in the first place. What follows is an account, by no means exhaustive, of why the world now moves in sneakers.

I am indebted to Matt Weiland and his colleagues at The New Press for having the foresight to pick the "once lowly sneaker" to inaugurate The Press's Bazaar Books series—a series that will get people thinking about the everyday products with which we surround ourselves. Trade periodicals such as *Sportstyle* provided helpful information, as did employees at a number of athletic shoe firms. Brian Kroll at Footwear Industries of America provided me with a wealth of statistical material, while Nathaniel Wice supported my efforts in various ways. Thanks must also go to my parents, for granting me my wish to own a pair of Nikes (and thus propelling a lasting fascination), and to Darcy, always willing to endure another draft.

1

Starting Blocks

A Short History of the Sneaker

"They're like hot dogs—part of America."
—*Newsweek*, 1962

The New Widget

CALL IT A SNEAKER, call it an athletic shoe. That lightweight bundle of polymer and plastic, leather and lace is more than just footwear. Follow its footprints carefully, for they run straight through the heart of American culture, across the global economy, and along the contours of contemporary history. In the consumer marketplace, few products in the past twenty years have had the kind of success—or profit margins—that sneakers have had. The numbers alone are staggering. In 1997, Americans bought nearly 350 million pairs of sneakers, or roughly one and a half for every member of the republic and one-fifth of the world's total. Athletic shoes were far and away the most popular shoe sold, commanding more than twice the market share of dress or "casual" shoes. The athletic shoe companies

A Timeline of Sneaker History

1836	U.S. inventor Charles Goodyear receives patent for vulcanized rubber
1868	Goodyear perfects the "vulcanization" process
1870	Word "sneak" defined by American lexicographer as "shoes with canvas tops and India rubber soles"
1876	Britain's New Liverpool Rubber Co. produces rubber-soled croquet shoe
1892	Nine companies merge to form U.S. Rubber Co.
1894	Thomas Bata launches Bata Shoes in Zlin, Czechoslovakia
1895	Joseph Foster founds Reebok in England
1906	New Balance Arch and Support Co. founded in Boston
1907	Converse Rubber Co. is formed in Malden, Massachusetts by Marquis M. Converse
1912	A.R. Hyde and Sons formed (later Hyde Athletic Industries, parent of Saucony and Spot-Bilt shoes, among others)
1914	Brooks Sports is formed

2

pull in over $11 billion a year in domestic retail sales (roughly twice that globally), while stock analysts are assigned to track the mercurial shifts of the "athletic footwear industry." The average price paid for a pair of sneakers is just a shade over thirty dollars, but sales of Nike footwear and apparel alone amount to an average of twenty dollars for every U.S. citizen. Companies such as Fila and Reebok dominate "brand recognition" studies among young consumers, while teenagers—many of whom knew the launch date in advance— line up to buy the latest release.

A vertiginously dynamic industry, based on an intense mixture of fashion, marketing, high-technology design, and low-technology labor, sneakers are like walking economic and cultural indicators. The sneaker has even been put forward as the new model product for classroom economics courses: the *Far Eastern Economic Review* posited that the "once lowly sports shoe—the end product of an increasingly complicated design, production,

3

1916 U.S. Rubber Co. produces Keds (mixture of "kids" and "ped")

1917 Converse Rubber Co. produces first "All-Star"

1920 Duke of Windsor spurs tennis shoe craze in U.S. visit

1923 Converse All-Stars logo embellished by name of company salesman and semi-pro basketball player Chuck Taylor

1924 British Olympic "Chariots of Fire" runners outfitted by Reebok

1924 The Dassler schufabrik opens in Germany

1936 Jesse Owens wears Dassler shoes in Berlin Olympics

1948 Dassler brothers split, forming Adidas and Puma

1950 Ventilating eyelets on sneaker sides introduced

1960 Puma pays West German Olympic runner Armin Hary to switch from Adidas

1962 New Balance introduces first wedge-heeled running shoe

and delivery process coordinating dozens of multinational companies under ever shorter deadlines—illustrates the realities of trade and globalization more clearly than the widget of classic economic texts ever did." One writer speaks of the "sneakerization" of the economy, where once simple, inexpensive goods such as sunglasses have multiplied—just as sneakers did before them—into highly segmented, rapid-turnover markets with endless product extensions playing on the power of brand equity and image building. The sneaker is the ultimate "soft good," the word economists use to describe products in which, as Benjamin Barber observes, "the trademark has surpassed the sales item and the image has overtaken the product as the key to earned income." Accordingly, sneaker companies have gone from being manufacturing-driven companies to marketing-driven companies. A 1950s study of sneaker maker Hood Rubber found that manufacturing costs accounted for nearly half of product costs, but by the 1990s the manufacturing costs of a pair of Nike Pegasus represented no more than 20 percent of the purchase price. The *Economist* waxes enthusiastic about "the Nike economy," using the company as a

1963 Adidas issues Stan Smith and Rod Laver tennis shoes

1964 Kihachiro Onitsuka forms Onitsuka Tiger, later ASICS Tiger

1966 Vans Rubber Co. formed in California; Converse "All-Star" adds seven colors to its two-tone line

1968 San Diego Rockets of ABA become first basketball team to wear Adidas shoes; Puma and Adidas pay athletes to wear shoes in Mexico City Olympics

1972 Philip Knight forms Blue Ribbon Sports, selling track shoes under the "Nike" brand; first Athlete's Foot and Athletic Attic stores open

1974 Puma releases the "Clyde," after Walt "Clyde" Frazier, the first basketball player to have his own shoe

1977 Kihachiro Onitsuka forms ASICS in Japan and the U.S.

1979 Stride-Rite Corp. buys "Keds" from Uniroyal; Nike Tailwind breaks fifty dollar price barrier paradigm for flexible, country-hopping "virtual organizations" built on a web of outsourcing and just-in-time production, or even the "Nike indicator," for the supposed relationship between the company's presence in an "Asian tiger" country and a subsequent rise in the country's standard of living. Yet the sneaker has also been at the center of a global battle between multinational corporations and activist groups over the rights and conditions of workers in those same countries.

The athletic shoe industry's impact spreads far beyond the economic realm. Now shoe companies are viewed as agents of social change, sparking fitness movements, "changing the game" of American advertising and merchandising, breaking down racial, class, and gender barriers (or, some would say, building them up). Nike pays over $40 million to associate its logo with Tiger Woods, the young golfer of mixed racial heritage, vaulting the color line of

1980	Nike pulls advertising from *Runner's World*, claiming bias in running shoe survey
1985	Nike releases first "Air Jordan" shoe
1986	ASICS introduces "gel" shoe; Run-D.M.C. records "My Adidas"
1987	Nike releases first "cross-trainer;" uses Beatles' "Revolution" in an advertisement
1990	First Nike Town opened in Portland, Oregon
1991	Reebok debuts the $170 "Pump" shoe; Italy's Fila company buys out U.S. licensee; L.A. Gear releases Lights, sneakers with glowing red lights in the rear
1992	Controversy erupts as Nike-endorsed U.S. Olympic basketball players refuse to wear team-sponsor Reebok warm-up suits
1997	Ex-Mayor of Atlanta Andrew Young tours Nike's Asian production facilities

THERE ARE ALMOST AS MANY NAMES FOR SNEAKERS AS THERE ARE BRANDS.

Snē-kər

Aerobic shoes	Plimsolls
Basketball boots	(U.K.)
Boat shoes	Outing shoes
Bobos	Runners
Boots	Sabogs
Bumper boots	Sandshoes
Cleats	Shoeclacks
Cross-trainers	Skiffs
Daps (Wales)	Sneaks
Deck shoes	Sneakers
Drug shoes	Soccer boots
Felony shoes	Speed shoes
Fishheads	Tackies
Football boots (U.K.)	(South Africa)
Go-fasters	Tennie-
Gym shoes	runners
Grapplers	Tennies
High-tops	Tennis shoes
Hoop shoes	Tetanus
Keds (India)	shoes
Kicks	Track shoes
Les Baskets,	Trainers
Les Trainings	(U.K.)
(France)	

Source: Charlie's Sneaker Pages
(www.sneakers.pair.com),
and author research.

the power elite's game of choice; Reebok, meanwhile, pays $3 million to Venus Williams, accomplishing the same thing in tennis. Reebok and Nike have become the prime sponsors of competing women's basketball leagues, challenging the male dominance of professional sports and opening new markets for their products. (While the number of athletic shoes sold has declined in this decade, sales of women's product have risen.) The shoes are pitched as tools of personal improvement, holding out hope to the consumer that they can be as good as the superstar who shares their brand. It is not just athletic improvement: one Nike spot shows a girl and flashes the caption "If you let me play, I will be more likely to leave a man who beats me." Sneakers confer status, spark discussion, spawn biomechanical sciences. Athletic shoes are to other shoes as sport-utility vehicles are to other cars: large, loaded with impressive but rarely used options, a statement less of need than desire.

Like the personal computer, the athletic shoe as we know it is a product of the last several decades. Indeed, in 1985, as the wave was beginning to crest for both products, Puma introduced the "RS Computer Shoe," a two-hundred-dollar running shoe that could be connected to one's Apple or Commodore computer and, using special software, record and process running data. It was considered a perfect marketing marriage for the then-novel "young urban professional" market: high-tech shoes meeting high-tech computers, soft wear paired with software, exercise turned into something more purposeful, more precise. Athletic pursuits were once considered leisure, but in the 1980s they were treated more like work, with careful accounting practices, rationalized systems for isolating and treating one part of the body at a time, and a bottom line-inspired focus on "results." The yuppie consumption ethos demanded status-defining niche products at every turn, scientific studies were trotted out showing how running shoes could combat "overpronation" and other syndromes (even if, as writer Edward Tenner points out, being able to run farther because of lighter, springier shoes might inadvertently put more strain on the knees), and just as personal computers were suddenly touted as the best way to balance a checkbook, athletic shoes became necessary equipment for running. Even the new computer and sneaker companies were similar: Microsoft and Nike, for example, were both based in the Pacific Northwest, had grown out of small start-up firms, featured extremely driven, visionary leaders (who, aptly enough, in the case of Bill Gates, Steven Jobs, and countless other programmer-CEOs, were noted for wearing running shoes) and young, hardcore employees—known cheekily as "microserfs" at the computer company and "Ekins" ("Nikes" spelled backward) at the shoe company.

In 1982, when my first pair of Nike's were well worn, approximately 183 million pairs of athletic shoes were sold. A decade later that number would double. A market that had been fractured between the simple canvas-and-rubber Keds for children and the early Tiger track shoes for dedicated runners would, in the span of a decade, come to unite a near majority of the population: adults and children, whites and blacks, couch potatoes and athletes alike. Sneakers went from yearly back-to-school requirements and innocent objects of nostalgia to the repositories of high hopes and hoop dreams, the totems of individual status, the building blocks of global brands, the foundation of a cult of personal fitness. Somewhere along the line, a shoe became a lifestyle. In that pair of sneakers lies a story of the convulsive social and cultural changes that have rippled through America in the past few decades, of the quicksilver reorganization of the global economy, of a fundamental shift in the relation between consumers and products.

First Steps

THE SNEAKER'S LONG MARCH starts in nineteenth-century England. Known as "sand shoes" or "plimsolls" (because the line on the shoe's foxing resembled the mark on a ship—named after British parliamentarian Samuel Plimsoll—indicating proper cargo weight), the shoes were a favorite for aristocratic lawn sports. Centuries earlier, accounts document Henry VIII wearing "shooys with feltys, to play in at Tennys" in 1517 and inhabitants of the Amazon donning gum-soled shoes crafted from the local supply ("gum shoes," as they were called, were later imported to the U.S.), but it was the American inventor Charles Goodyear's patented vulcanization process in 1839—and his subsequent refinements—that made the modern sneaker possible. In *Female Life in Prison*, published in England in 1862, we learn that "the night officer is generally accustomed to wear a species of India-rubber shoes or galoshes on her feet. These are termed 'sneaks' by the women [of Brixton prison]." In 1870, American etymologist James Greenwood's *In Strange Company* describes "sneaks" as "shoes with canvas tops and india rubber soles." The word is generally associated with cat burglars or "sneak thieves." By 1897, tennis shoes were listed in the Sears catalog at $0.60 a pair.

By the early 1900s, the sneaker industry was a viable if small concern, concentrated in a number of northeastern rubber companies whose specialty was bicycle tires (soon to be auto-mobile tires). U.S. Rubber, formed from nine smaller rubber-products firms in 1892, introduced Keds in 1916, while Converse, a rubber footwear manufacturer founded in Malden, Massachusetts in 1908 by Marquis M. Converse, produced the first "All-Star" in 1917. A number of other companies, including B.F. Goodrich and A.G. Spalding Co., were also making sneakers, including basketball and tennis shoes, while family-run companies such as Brooks and Etonic (named after Charles Eaton) were manufacturing early versions of cleated sports shoes. Sneakers were already a global business: the rubber that went into them came largely from Brazil, and then Indonesia, as companies such as Goodyear bought plantations there to undercut the Brazilian cartels.

The sneaker market, at first so small as to warrant virtually no mention in the national press, expanded quickly after World War I as more Americans turned to sports and physical health. The upper classes, once suspicious of mass sport, sought to channel its energy, and moralists and reformers touted the "strenuous life" as the fiber of the national character and sport a demonstration of the country's burgeoning imperial greatness. As it would be later in the century, the public's enchantment with sport was firmly grounded in consumer culture. The historians Elliot Gorn and Warren Goldstein, writing in *A Brief History of American Sports*, note that, "to purchase leisure—to be a spectator at a great event, for example, or buy a bicycle or a baseball mitt—was to participate in an even more important part of American culture: the consumption of goods produced by others."

The sneaker market grew steadily, if quietly, through the next few decades. In the U.S., young boys were the prime purchasers of B.F. Goodrich's line of "Chief Long Lance" sports shoes endorsed by Jim Thorpe; and the Converse All-Star, which in 1923 became the signature shoe of Charles "Chuck" Taylor, a semi-pro basketball player and

company salesman who toured the country, putting on clinics and selling shoes (a WorldCom ad would later hint that part of Michael Jordan's endorsement contract meant he had to actually perform work for the company, but in Chuck Taylor's prehistoric era of celebrity endorsement, it was no joke). In the 1920s and 1930s, companies added traction to soles, advertised different shoes for different sports, and produced distinct models for boys and girls (none of this, however, hinted at the dizzying diversification that would hit the market in the 1980s). The shoes were known for their comfort, but there was relatively little else to it, save for the occasional fashion concern: E. B. White wrote in 1942 that the "question of what to wear is always baffling. From *Harper's Bazaar*, which is my Bible, I learn that the Boston group in New Haven frown on new garments in their summer colony, and that a man in a new pair of sneakers is snubbed." A half-century later, White would more likely have fretted over sneakers that were too old.

At the beginning of the twentieth century, several pioneering companies were advancing in Europe as well, fueled by a rising interest in athletics, particularly the revived Olympic Games, which seemed to grow in popularity as political tensions across Europe heightened in the 1930s. In England, starting in 1900, Joseph Foster produced Reebok shoes (worn by the runners depicted in the hit 1983 film *Chariots of Fire*). In Herzogenaurach, Germany, a young entrepreneur named Adolf Dassler began making shoes bearing his surname from World War I scrap and surplus; in 1928, his shoes debuted at the Olympic Games in Amsterdam, and in 1936 a Dassler-clad Jesse Owens captured four gold medals and stood defiantly before Hitler. (More than fifty years later, the source of controversy at the Olympics,

Adidas
1996 sales: $1,742,000,000

The Dassler dynasty began in 1926 when brothers Adolf and Rudi opened a football-shoe factory in the small German shoe-making town of Herzogenaurach. Their shoes were soon being worn by Olympic athletes, most famously Jesse Owens in the 1936 Olympics in Berlin. In 1946, after a simmering feud split the brothers for good, Adolf created the firm of Adidas (after a contraction of his name), based in his house, employing forty-seven workers and crafting shoes out of U.S. military surplus materials. The company soon rose to prominence in soccer and Olympic circles, helped along by technical innovations such as the replaceable cleat. By the late 1960s, Adidas had sixteen factories, which together produced twenty-two thousand pairs of shoes a day, and had a near-total lock on the Olympics and FIFA, the international governing body for soccer. In the 1970s, the

11

"brand with the three stripes" had eclipsed Converse as the leading seller of athletic shoes in the United States, only to be overtaken by Nike soon after Adolf's death in 1978. As nimble competitors Nike, Reebok, and Fila signed sports stars and boosted ad budgets, Adidas fell out of touch with the vital U.S. market. After Adolf's son Horst died in 1987, Adidas was purchased by the French politician and entrepreneur Bernard Tapie, who became embroiled in a web of corruption charges three years later and was forced to give up the company to Crédit Lyonnaise. Adidas was bought at fire-sale prices by ex-Saachi and Saachi chairman Robert Louis-Dreyfus. In the last several years, Adidas has closed many of its European production facilities, expanded its U.S. presence, and increased sponsorship activity, signing NBA draftee Kobe Bryant and paying an estimated $40 million to sponsor the 1998 World Cup.

in Barcelona, would be the shoes themselves, as a group of U.S. basketball players demanded to wear the logo of their corporate sponsor.) After a wartime interruption in which shoe factories across the world converted to military production (for example, Converse produced the U.S. Air Force's A6 flying boot, while the Dassler factory was converted by the Wehrmacht to make army boots), sneakers began a renewed, slow ascendance, aided by a postwar rise in the popularity of basketball. In Germany, 1948, Rudi Dassler (who spent time after the war in a POW camp) formed the Puma company after a feud with brother Adolf, whose Adidas brand was to emerge as the dominant force in athletics, the shoe of choice of soccer players and Olympians, and eventually, basketball players. In Kobe, Japan, in the 1950s, Kihachiro Onitsuka began making basketball shoes in his living room— the beginning of an enterprise that would ultimately become ASICS Tiger. Meanwhile, Bata, which was founded in Czechoslovakia but was later headquartered in Canada, had emerged as the world's largest shoe exporter, and sneakers numbered high among its products in markets such as Malaysia.

In the 1950s, the American sneaker market saw the first of several "takeoffs." With families flocking to the suburbs, leisure time and sports participation on an upward slope, and the Baby Boom beginning to coalesce, sneakers—the word still meant canvas and rubber—were becoming the shoe of choice for American youth. As Jonathan Walford, curator of the Bata Shoe Museum in Toronto, observes, the sneaker was an integral part of the first distinctly marketed youth fashion and cultural movement in American history. As school dress codes began to relax, the sneaker also became acceptable for daily wear, although, as he points out, "You would have had two pairs: one for school and one for gym class." With James Dean sporting Jack Purcells and the Jets and Sharks of *West Side Story* clad in sneakers—more foreshadowing, this time of L.A.'s blood and Crips buying particular brands and colors in the 1980s and 90s—sneakers, like blue jeans and rock and roll, were hallmarks of youth hip.

In 1962, *The New Yorker* was moved to inform its readers about a "revolution that seems to be taking place in footgear." Sales of the "once lowly sneaker," the magazine noted, had more than doubled in the past six years. Indeed, sales had soared from 35 million a decade previous to 130 million the year before, to over 150 million pairs by May 1962—a big splash in a domestic shoe market that had held steady at 600 million pairs annually

Airwalk

1996 sales: $225,000,000

Positioned as the "anti-Nike," and boasting such high-profile customers as R.E.M.'s Michael Stipe, this Altoona, Pennsylvania-based sneaker company has risen within a decade from an obscure, $11 million-a-year concern into a $240 million-plus sensation. Founded in 1986, Airwalk was the brainchild of George Yohn and Bill Mann, who has since gone to competitor Vans. Named after the skateboard-popping maneuver, Airwalk shoes were designed with foot-dragging and other skateboarding moves in mind; the brand was initially perceived as a statement against the jockish performance fetishism of the big brands. An early 1990s skateboarding backlash, in which many of the nation's parks were closed for insurance, curfew, and other reasons, almost sank Airwalk: sales dwindled to $8 million. But just as Nike succeeded in selling athletic shoes to non-athletes,

Airwalk succeeded in selling skateboarding, snowboarding, BMX, and other types of shoes to sedentary, yet "extreme" sports-minded consumers. Soon, Airwalk's line—filled out with fuzzy yellow and shiny plastic sneakers, fleece-lined rubberized clogs, and retro "Jim Shoes"—was appearing next to the major brands in the malls. In the mid-1990s, Airwalk next moved into "brown shoes" it deemed more suitable for the college-aged set than the company's original audience.

since 1957. Leather shoe manufacturers responded with campaigns claiming that sneakers were bad for children's feet (a warning that haunted a generation), and targeted teens with print ads that advised, "A Leather Shoe Brings Out the Real You." Undaunted, the sneaker manufacturers fought back with equally puffy claims that sneakers helped cure the syndrome of "inhibited feet," which one magazine wryly described as a "psychosomatic ailment, hitherto unknown to us, that is supposed to lead to mental depression." Companies even began making sneakers endowed with pseudoscientific enhancements, such as the P.F. ("Posture Foundation") Flyer. Television ads for such sneakers as U.S. Rubber's "U.S. Keds" highlighted the "shock-proof arch cushion," while a puckish animated clown named "Kedso" asked children why they wore Keds ("So I can run faster and jump farther" was a typical response).

The sneaker was on its way to becoming an icon. "They're socially acceptable now," a U.S. Rubber official told *Newsweek* that same week. "They're like hot dogs—part of America." Yet even if they were viewed as quintessentially American, there were hints on the horizon that they would not always be of American origin. By 1961, long before anyone had heard of a Toyota, the U.S. was importing 28 million pairs of sneakers from Japan. "The Japanese haven't provided anything but cheap merchandise," an executive from B.F. Goodrich, makers of P.F. Flyers, told *Newsweek*. It was a harbinger of things to come for the sneaker and American manufacturing in general.

Goodrich rode the sneaker boom well, and its P.F. Flyer commanded 18.7 percent of the market in 1964. As the foreign competition increased, Goodrich pursued a soon-to-be familiar path. It moved its footwear operations from Massachusetts to lower-wage Puerto Rico and Lumberton, South Carolina—where it "beat back" an attempt by the United Rubber Workers union to organize. A tariff protecting U.S.-made rubber-soled footwear was overturned in 1966, and Goodrich's shoe division limped along for several years before being purchased by the same holding company that had purchased Converse a year before. The intensifying youth culture of the postwar boom demanded new styles at an ever-increasing rate, shepherded along by a global economic system that saw planned obsolescence and changes in fashion as a way to keep consumption in step with increased productivity and technological innovation on the production side. The technology of sports shoes themselves was rapidly changing (the metal molds for soles, for example, were changing yearly, and new processes such as compression molding replaced the long-standing method of vulcanization). It was all too much for a standard, Fordist industrial operation like Goodrich, with its high fixed costs and long production runs. Just as the dress and casual shoe industries were

Bata

1996 sales: Not available

Now headquartered in Canada, Bata Shoes was founded by Tomas Bata in 1894 in the town of Zlin, Czechoslovakia. Bata was one of the first mass-assembly shoe manufacturers, producing over two thousand pairs a day by 1905, and by the 1930s it was the world's largest shoe exporter. Bata became known for establishing factories in overlooked corners of the developing world (well before the arrival of companies like Adidas, Nike, or Reebok), building factories in India, Cyprus, Lebanon, the Ivory Coast, and other locales at a rate averaging two per year until the 1960s (various factories were nationalized in the Eastern Bloc and other Communist nations). It has mostly maintained its reputation for fair labor practices, often paying workers several times the rate offered by Asian subcontractors, and its basic canvas sneakers and other shoes are a favorite outside of the industrialized West; its

15

"bubblegummers" brand, or example, is the number one children's sneaker in Mexico and Thailand. The company also introduced various vulcanization and manufacturing innovations in athletic shoes. Bata, which is still family owned and privately held, maintains a network of more than four thousand retail outlets in various countries under different names. Revenues are estimated to be $3 billion annually. In the mid-1990s, Bata's profits began to slip as newer, marketing-driven shoe companies established footholds in territory long held by Bata, and the company underwent a financial restructuring.

being rocked by foreign competition (imports, one percent of the industry in 1955, accounted for 21 percent of the market in 1968; while employment in the New England shoe industry was cut nearly in half between 1960 and 1974), before long only a handful of companies would be producing sneakers domestically. In 1968, American companies were worrying about Adidas' penetration into the U.S. (the shoes were made in Germany, which now has the world's highest manufacturing wages but certainly didn't then), and from the first half of 1972 to the first half of 1973, sneaker imports had risen 25 percent. The future of the industry had been presaged in a 1972 Nike advertisement. "Designed with the athlete in mind," the ad boasted, "Nike is not bound by tradition or long, profitable production runs." In another spot, it compared itself to Volkswagen, and just as Detroit would later be caught napping as smaller, imported cars caught on, so too would the "limousines for the feet," as Converse billed their shoes, be eclipsed by flashier, foreign-produced footwear.

Sneaking into the Seventies

"Jogging," the *New York Times Magazine* said in a May 1968 cover story, "seems on its way to becoming the new 'in' sport." The article is noteworthy less for its observations on how the age of automation was creating a need for exercise apart from work than for the fact that, in the course of several thousand words, there was not one mention of shoes. Contrast that to today, when choosing the "right" pair of shoes is considered the first step in running; when splashy, full-color ads from Nike and New Balance equate running with an improved life ("You can run to become a better runner," reads one ad, "Or you can run to become better"); and when shoes, derived from aero-space-industry technology and "wear tested" in bio-mechanical research labs, are considered catalysts in one's alchemical transformation into budding Olympian. Looking at the $600 million-plus running shoe (to say nothing of the running apparel) industry today, *BusinessWeek* would no doubt be impressed, having noted in 1979 that, "if any sport should present hurdles to sportswear suppliers, it is probably running, which is more solitary than social, and there is scant need for equipment."

The need, it turned out, could be created. Through "lifestyle marketing," in which a product becomes a sort of personality extension, one could market a shoe for just about anything—even walking. Today, it is hard to imagine that just over twenty years ago the logos of athletic shoe companies were not ubiquitously emblazoned on the nation's shirts, shoes, and sweat-pants; conversely, twenty years ago it would have been

Converse

1996 sales: $642,000,000

Founded in 1908 by Marquis M. Converse, the former manager of a New England rubber shoe company, the Converse Rubber Shoe Co. moved—like most rubber companies—into automobile tires. For Converse, it proved disastrous, and the company plunged into receivership in 1928. But not before it issued, in 1917, the "All-Star"—later known as the "Chuck Taylor" (after a company salesman who traveled the country putting on basketball clinics). By the 1930s, under the ownership of a local family, the Malden, Massachusetts-based Converse had carved out a niche selling its shoes in sporting goods stores since it was blocked from department stores by the big rubber companies. By the 1960s, Converse was the dominant sneaker company, its shoe worn by nearly every professional basketball player. But by the next decade, Converse was struggling to keep up with Adidas, Nike, and other new companies who

rolled out new styles and technologies yearly. In 1986, Converse was acquired by Interco, a St. Louis-based manufacturer. The 1980s saw the company climb back, bolstered by its Dr. J–Larry Bird ad campaign and a retro revival of the Chuck Taylor. In 1994, Converse became an independent company and is one of the few sneaker companies to retain a U.S. manufacturing presence.

unthinkable that a player paid to endorse a sneaker might earn more than the combined yearly wages of the workers who produced it. The story of the rise of sneakers is inherently tied to a more fundamental story: the dramatic rise of commercialism.

From 1950 to 1990, or from P.F. Flyers to the Reebok Pump, global ad spending has risen from $39 billion to $256 billion, a third faster than the expansion of the world economy and seven times faster than world population growth. The licensing industry's revenues, another telling indicator, soared from under $5 billion a year in 1977 to more than $66 billion in 1990.

Sneaker companies, meanwhile, went from production-minded concerns that rolled out the same lines for decades to marketing-minded firms working under the assumption of planned obsolescence. Early on, athletic shoe repair services advertised in places like *Runner's World* and refurbishing compounds such as Shoe Goo were sold, but eventually, as with many consumer goods, the response was: Just chuck it. The rise of global media helped speed the flow of styles, while television revenues helped turn sports into big business. In 1973, according to Donald Katz's *Just Do It,* Nike, which now pays over $70 million combined to Michael Jordan and Tiger Woods, had an athlete promotion program that consisted of sending an employee "to hang around the gyms at UCLA and USC to try and give away a few pairs of shoes." Fila wasn't even in the market until the 1990s, and yet by 1997 it was paying Grant Hill $80 million to wear its product.

Sneakers were not merely less popular in 1968, when jogging was headed our way; their producers hadn't quite yet figured out what could be done with them. Shoes were still shoes. An article on Adidas shoe production in 1974 led off by declaring that "most people's interest in athletics includes just the athletes themselves or the team on which they play." Not what the players are wearing. In the beginning of the 1970s, however, the sneaker was already moving on to bigger things. The culture of athlete endorsement, for one, was on the rise, even before 1970. At the 1968 Mexico City Olympics, Adidas and Puma were embroiled in a controversy over paying track athletes to wear their shoes, a policy Puma had initiated in 1960, when it paid the West German track star Armin Hary to bolt from Adidas. A handful of U.S. basketball players and other athletes had been paid marginal amounts to wear shoes in the 1950s and 1960s. Where the signature shoe had largely been limited to tennis, in the early 1970s Converse named a shoe after baseball star Lou Brock and Puma created the low-cut suede "Clyde" after the New York Knicks' guard Walt Frazier. As Frazier later

Fila

1996 sales: $830,000,000

Fila is an Italian fashion company, founded in 1926 by Dr. Enrico Frachey, which first broke U.S. ground in the 1970s with its Bjorn Borg–endorsed line of tennis wear. In the following decade Fila, like Gucci and Louis Vuitton, became an "aspirational brand" in the inner city; rappers donned Fila tracksuits in symbolic homage to the good life, and even the company's modest sneaker brand began to make inroads. In the 1990s, Fila has sought to stress athletic performance over its inner-city fashion image. The Dallas Mavericks' Jamal Mashburn became Fila's first shoe endorser in 1993; the Detroit Pistons' Grant Hill joined forces with Fila the following year and put the company in the major leagues when his signature shoe sold 1.5 million units (it was the most popular line since Air Jordans). Fila's market-share doubled in two years, and it vaulted into third place in the U.S. sneaker market; meanwhile, the Fila logo had become an icon among style-obsessed eighties revivalists. In 1997, as the company's shoe sales began to lag, Fila continued to expand its hip-hop fashion niche by hiring three designers from the streetwear firm Mecca USA to head up its ENYCE ("phonetic" spelling of the letters NYC) label.

told the *Wall Street Journal*, "there wasn't a lot of hoopla. I was just proud knowing I was the only guy getting paid to have my name on a shoe." Within a few years Julius Erving had a similar deal, but was getting the now inconceivably low sum of twenty-five thousand dollars.

The athletic shoe industry was reinventing itself yearly. In 1973 *Runner's World*, the bible of the nascent running movement, wrote that the running shoe industry, once a fairly static entity dominated by Adidas, "is the scene of so much upheaval that it's hard to keep up with thechanges." Japan's Tiger, Germany's Puma, America's New Balance and Nike (only one year old, but brashly calling itself "the shoe for the seventies") were suddenly populating the pages of the magazine with new models and new materials. In basketball, where Converse had long held a near monopoly over players' footwear, Puma, Pony, and most dramatically, Adidas, were starting to grace a few feet. Shoes that were not sneakers in the traditional sense—that is, shoes that were lighter and perhaps intended for specific athletic purposes, began filtering through popular culture. Sneaker marketing now touted athletic performance and fashion: an ad for Bata Bullets, for example, claimed one could lead "two lives" in the shoes, which had "special features for playing sports" yet were also "styled great for casual wear." The shoes of the Baby Boom were suddenly every-where, but they bore exotic names and were made of strange materials. In 1974, *Footwear News* noted that "no longer are sneakers a money-saving entity for customers. Leather sneakers are more expensive than the highest-priced oxford. But they have taken on a fashion appeal, and the kids will want them no matter what the price." The sneaker could be an all-American pop icon, or a bold statement of countercultural casualness. The Adidas "trefoil," meanwhile, designed to add copyright protection to the company's three-striped shoes, was showing up everywhere from T-shirts to equipment bags—thanks to a major boost from Adidas' dominance at the Mexico City Olympics. Woody Allen wore sneakers to the ballet, one could spot Adidas Gazelles peppered throughout such films as the Led Zeppelin documentary *The Song Remains the Same* (1976), while in *All the President's Men* (1976) Dustin Hoffman, playing the Washington Post reporter Carl Bernstein, wore them in the office. In 1971, the Kinney company commissioned the pop artist Peter Max to design a line of sneakers, presumably building on the same pop appeal Roy Lichtenstein had seized upon in his 1961 still life *Keds*. Sneaker advertising, taking its cues from the "creative revolution" of the 1960s, grew looser and began constructing identity around the shoes. A Converse "Limousines for Your Feet" spot showed a young basketball player reading a poem in front of his classmates. Walford, of the Bata Shoe Museum, points to an early 1970s ad that showed a Bata-clad teenager lying on his back, legs crossed and

Hi-Tec

1996 sales: Not available

Billed as Britain's largest domestic sneaker producer and the seventh largest brand worldwide, Hi-Tec was established in Essex, England, in 1974. The Hi-Tec "Squash" was an early success (eventually selling some nine million pairs worldwide), and the company eventually eclipsed rival Dunlop and its beloved "Green Flash" (which, like Keds, was enjoying a bit of a revival in the 1990s among pop stars and others). Hi-Tec went public in 1988 and in 1994 became partners with Dutch-owned Vilenzo. Hi-Tec, which produces its shoes in Asia as well as Rumania, saw its market share erode in the 1990s and has countered by venturing further into the "rugged casuals" market.

Keds

1996 sales: $286,000,000

Along with the All-Star or the P.F. Flyer, Keds is the quintessential American sneaker of the twentieth-century. Launched in 1916 after the U.S. Rubber Co decided to consolidate its numerous styles into one shoe, the white-canvas, blue-label Keds (a mixture of "kids" and "ped") were a perennial favorite of youth—especially children—for most of the century. In the 1970s, Keds was overtaken by more expensive, more heavily marketed sneakers. In 1979, the Cambridge, Massachusetts-based Stride-Rite Corp. purchased Keds, which had been losing $20 million annually, from Uniroyal for $10.5 million. The company's first efforts to revive the brand failed; a leather "Pro-Keds" line for athletes fizzled and was dropped in 1986, as did a fifty-dollar running shoe. By the mid-1980s, after it had noticed a market developing for cheaper, nonathletic sneakers, Keds had repositioned

22

listening to music. The shoes, the ad suggested, were part of a "cool" lifestyle.

Shoe advertisements began featuring individual athletes, such as Chris Evert Lloyd, a trend related to another surge of the country's interest in sports. In 1973, *Fortune* said of tennis that "a once clubby sport is becoming a national pastime," with the market growing by some $500 million a year. (Pros such as Rod Laver and Stan Smith, who each had their own shoe since the 1960s, were forerunners of the celebrity endorsers to come.) In 1975, *U.S. News & World Report* reported that "Americans in record numbers are turning to some form of physical activity for recreation."

In 1975, the country spent nearly $6.2 billion on sports equipment—not including shoes—up 21 percent in only two years. In 1976, Jim Fixx added more horsepower to the high-revving jogging craze with *The Book of Running*, and the celebrity workout trend was not far behind. Perhaps more importantly, attendance levels at spectator sports soared as well. Pro basketball, for one, saw a 240 percent rise in attendance from 1965 to 1974. Free agency was entering professional sports, and a cult of merchandising around celebrity athletes was developing: Yankee outfielder Reggie Jackson's "Reggie Bar" was just an appetizer.

The shoes themselves were technologically upgraded with the introduction of new lightweight materials and foam composites; Bill Bowerman's "waffle sole" and Nike "Air" turned shoe attributes into commodities themselves. The shoes were better than they had been, in terms of weight and cushioning, and by the 1980s, athletic shoes set the comfort standard for all shoes. The sneakers that were bad for you were now orthopedic instruments to combat overpronation and other newfound maladies. Yet comfort alone rarely sells clothing of any kind. "I call it the Bruce Jenner mentality," a shoe store employee told the *Washington Post* in 1978. "Jenner runs well in shoes, maybe I'll run better in them, too, is the way a lot of people figure." A cult of athleticism had developed, as it had at the turn of the century, but this time it was more personal than patriotic. Jogging, like self-help routines and New Age religions, was one of the activities critic Christopher Lasch singled out as indicative of a "culture of narcissism" into which a generation weary of the 1960s' political clashes was retreating (going, in Todd Gitlin's phrase, from j'accuse to jacuzzi). Lasch wrote, "People busy themselves instead with survival strategies, measures designed to prolong their own lives, or programs guaranteed to ensure good health and peace of mind."

Or, as a Nike marketer is quoted as saying in *Just Do It*, "One thing that all consumers share is a fear of death. [N]ike rose up by force of that fear and a host of other longings that seemed universal." The Boomers

the sneaker as a sensible shoe for women and children, and it upped the range of colors for wardrobe coordination. Sales rose from $60 million in 1986 to $227 million in 1989, as Keds appeared in fashion magazines and were extolled in lifestyle marketing campaigns. In 1997, Keds, hoping again to revitalize the brand, hired the fashion designer Todd Oldham to produce a line of fashion-conscious sneakers.

New Balance

1996 sales: $405,000,000

The New Balance Arch Company dates back to 1906, when William J. Riley found a niche making orthopedic shoes and arch supports out of a factory in Watertown, Massachusetts. The company turned to athletic shoes in the 1960s after runners started asking the company to craft special shoes. By 1972, the year it was purchased by its current owner, Jim Davis, New Balance's primary business was running shoes (six people making about thirty pairs of "Trackster" running shoes daily). New Balance got a boost in 1976 when its "320" model took first place in the annual *Runner's World* survey, and since then it has positioned itself as a serious maker of width-sensitive running shoes (the company branched into basketball in an expensive way in 1982, when it paid James Worthy to wear its shoes, but it soon returned solely to running). Along with Saucony,

were entering adulthood and beginning a race, as it were, against the clock. Shoes would become essential equipment in that race: during the second half of the decade Nike's sales shot up from $10 million to $270 million. If the ads for such shoes had initially been simple affairs showing the product, they would soon be elaborate, existentially tinged uplift banners that showed solitary runners on country roads (car ads promised a similar freedom) with tag lines like "There is no finish line." It is no accident that *The Big Chill* (1983), which traced the shift from political activism to personal atavism in a group of boomers, featured a character who had amassed his fortune selling jogging shoes. It is also no accident that four years later Nike would use two 1960s anthems—the Beatles' "Revolution" and John Lennon's "Instant Karma"— as background music to a collage of Nike-shod athletes.

The "Bruce Jenner mentality" (later to become the "Be Like Mike" mentality) was anchored to a desire for status-defining high-technology goods, and suddenly what you wore on your feet was more than utilitarian or even a "fashion statement." Whether the shoe companies drove or merely profited from the turn toward personal athleticism in the 1970s, they would not perfect the art of selling shoes (and apparel) on pure emotional aura until the 1980s, when shoe-company commercials would be repeated, parodied, acted out; when logos would appear without identification; when participation in almost any sport would require a panoply of branded equipment; when the president of Airwalk, an upstart Pennsylvania-based sneaker manufacturer, would be able to say, "We don't position ourselves as a shoe company. We're a marketing company that happens to sell shoes."

Air Apparent

In the 1980s, the faddish running shoe blossomed into the default footwear of a good share of the country's feet. (See Figures 2 and 3.) People still called them "sneakers" (to the dismay of marketers), but the old rubber company offspring were largely the stuff of memory; the parent companies closed or attempted to diversify into splashier lines. The Stride-Rite Corp., for example, which had purchased the Keds brand from Uniroyal Inc. in 1979, lost $7 million in the 1980–81 fiscal year, in part because its $50 "Millennium" performance shoe flopped. Industry analysts invented the term "athleisure" to account for shoes that fell between categories. The Adidas and Converse stronghold on the market was shattered. Nike and Reebok took over, and newer companies, including L.A. Gear and British Knights, gained ground. As the running shoe market tapered off, and companies like Brooks filed for Chapter 11, the shoe was getting new life from two sources. One was aerobics, which took off in the early 1980s and quickly became the exercise of choice for women. Reebok, a British company which then only had a small offshoot in the United States, looked to grab a piece of that market with the "Classic," a white shoe made of soft, somewhat wrinkled leather that was decidedly "fashion" oriented—which, in shoe industry speak, meant it did not have fancy cushioning and stability systems. The "Classic," doled out to aerobics instructors, proved such a hit that Reebok's sales rocketed from $3.5 million in 1982 to roughly $200 million in 1985 (its stock rose from $13 to $85 a share), knocking Nike out of first place and becoming, it was claimed, the fastest growing company in U.S. history.

The second trend keeping sneakers on the shelves was the rising popularity of basketball, which, thanks to marketable superstars such as Larry Bird and Julius Erving, was becoming a more television-friendly game—though even as late as the mid-1980s the majority of teams

FIGURE 2 *Athletic Shoes Sold in the U.S., 1982–95*

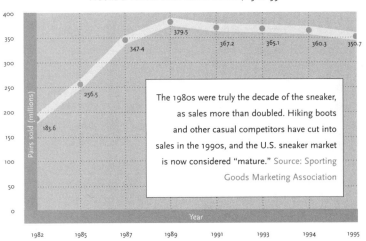

The 1980s were truly the decade of the sneaker, as sales more than doubled. Hiking boots and other casual competitors have cut into sales in the 1990s, and the U.S. sneaker market is now considered "mature." Source: Sporting Goods Marketing Association

still lost money and the league ranked low in the hierarchy of professional sports. Shoe companies were just beginning to grasp the possibility of marketing a player's personality; Nike's "Chocolate Thunder" Darryl Dawkins' poster is an early example. Nike, which launched an endorsement blitz in the NBA in the late 1970s, spreading money around even to reserve players, was shelling out $26 million a year to basketball players by 1983, more "than any ten sneaker companies put together," as one analyst noted. While endorsement money was much more widely distributed among players than it is today, the stakes even for top players was small

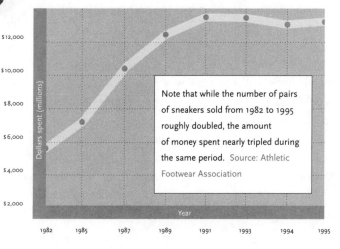

FIGURE 3 *Dollars Spent on Athletic Shoes in the U.S., 1982–95*

Note that while the number of pairs of sneakers sold from 1982 to 1995 roughly doubled, the amount of money spent nearly tripled during the same period. Source: Athletic Footwear Association

Dollars spent (millions)

$12,000
$10,000
$8,000
$6,000
$4,000
$2,000

Year

1982 1985 1987 1989 1991 1993 1994 1995

Nike

1996 sales: $5,008,000,000

The world's largest athletic shoe company sprang from modest origins: a former member of the University of Oregon track team, Phil "Buck" Knight, convinced Adidas' longstanding market lockhold could be broken, wrote a business school paper outlining his vision and soon after (in the mid-1960s) was selling Japan's Onitsuka Tiger track shoes out of his trunk. Aided by Oregon track coach and co-investor Bill Bowerman's "waffle sole" and other technical innovations, Blue Ribbon Sport's "Nike" shoes debuted in 1972 and were a word-of-mouth favorite. The company, based in Beaverton, Oregon, became known for its freewheeling, anti-authority ethos, thumbing its nose at athletic institutions (run by those whom Knight called the "sportocrats"). By the end of the decade, Nike was expanding aggressively into basketball and other sports, spending liberally on athlete endorsements, and by the early

1980s it surpassed Adidas in the United States. After missing the Reebok-driven aerobics boom, Nike rebounded with its "Air" line and has since continued to grow exponentially, now controlling over 40 percent of the market. Known as much for its brash advertising and business prowess as its expensive shoes, Nike has been able to transform its shoes into the foundation of a global entertainment brand, even while encountering criticism for the labor policies of its Pacific Rim subcontractors.

by today's standards: in 1982, the only basketball player worth six figures in sponsorship money was the Los Angeles Lakers center, Kareem Abdul-Jabbar, who received one hundred thousand dollars from Adidas. Later that year, however, the All-American James Worthy, the first-round draft pick of Jabbar's Lakers, signed a $1.2 million contract with New Balance to wear an eponymous shoe for the next eight years. The following year, Puma paid Ralph Sampson a similar amount to step out of his Pro-Keds. As *Sports Illustrated* put it, "Worthy's and Sampson's contracts threw the top of the scale out of whack," since more recognized players— Larry Bird, for example—were making no more than one hundred thousand dollars. Companies smelled the money in basketball, and new sneaker makers such as Kangaroos and Jordache wanted in.

Neither sneakers, basketball, nor the business world would be quite the same after Nike signed Michael Jordan in 1984. Jordan, despite his numerous college ball accolades, was picked third in the 1983 draft and was by no means an assured franchise player. But freshly bedecked with Olympic gold, likable, and telegenic, Jordan seemed capable of delivering basketball to the entire country. With this possibility in mind, and because Nike was anxious to enlist a showcase basketball endorser, Pro-Serv agent David Falk was able to wring from Nike the largest basketball endorsement deal then signed—roughly $2.5 million over five years. The tenuousness of the deal was marked, *Sports Illustrated* observed,

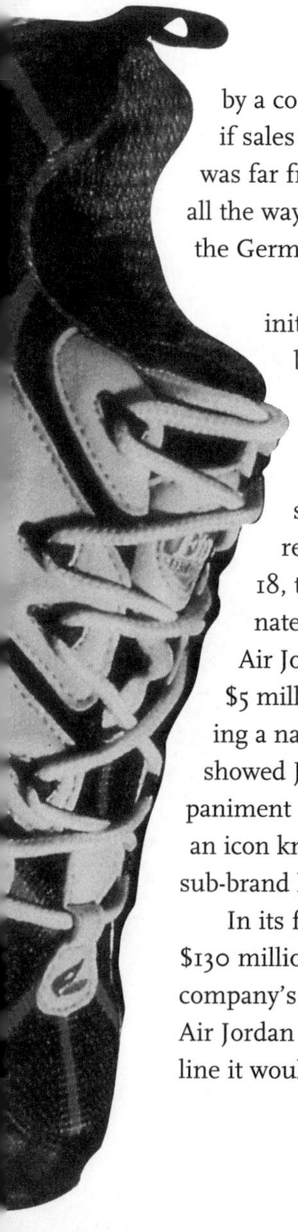

by a contract clause that would allow Nike to back out if sales weren't sufficient. (A further hint that the deal was far from a foregone conclusion was the rumor that all the way to the end, the Adidas-wearing Jordan hoped the German company would match Nike's offer.)

In 1984, Jordan began wearing "Air Jordans"—initially another model of Nike shoes colored red, black, and white. The Chicago Bulls and the NBA forced Jordan to wear shoes in the team's colors—red and white—and Nike played the ensuing controversy to the hilt: one spot intoned, "On October 15, Nike created a revolutionary new basketball shoe. On October 18, the NBA threw them out of the game. Fortunately, the NBA can't keep you from wearing them. Air Jordans. For Nike." That ad was just the first in a $5 million campaign over the next three years, including a nationally televised commercial in 1984 that showed Jordan leaping toward the basket to the accompaniment of a jet engine. The outline of a leaping Jordan, an icon known as "the Jump Man," would become a sub-brand logo as recognizable as Nike's swoosh.

In its first year, the Air Jordan line accounted for $130 million of Nike's sales and spurred the ailing company's comeback. As *Sports Illustrated* pointed out, Air Jordan sales were such that if it were an independent line it would be the fifth-largest athletic shoe company in

Puma

1996 sales: $375,000,000

After a legendary feud with his brother Adolf, who went on to found Adidas, Rudi Dassler created the Puma company in 1948, across town from his sibling rival in Herzogenaurach, Germany. By 1950, Puma had established export ties to the United States. Over the next several decades the brothers' battle would take place in the sports shoe arena, and with arms-race intensity they sought to get their shoes on the feet of the world's athletes. The drive to market new technologies spawned numerous copyright infringement lawsuits, and in 1960 Puma—trailing Adidas in sales by a nine-to-one ratio—opened a Pandora's box by paying the West German track star Armin Hary to defect over to the Puma side. Puma had a number of successes: its "King" soccer shoe worn by Eusebio in the 1968 World Cup, or its "Suede," (later the "Clyde") worn the same year by Black Power runners

America. Across the industry, basketball shoes had new cachet, and companies increased the range of shoes available, introduced gadgets ranging from velcro straps to plastic clamps to pumps, and stepped up their promotional efforts among professional and college athletes (and, more informally, on the street hoops level). By 1984, Nike and others were sponsoring summer basketball camps (known as "shoe camps") and making verbal agreements to outfit high school teams exclusively with their product. It was socially conscious marketing: providing organized outlets for playing and equipment in areas that often lacked both (a role that had once been limited to progressive-era institutions like the YMCA), while at the same time building brand loyalty from the ground up, using kids, as shoe camp maven Sonny Vacarro would later describe it, as "pawns" in a marketing war. Shaquille O'Neal, one of the NBA's endorsement machines and a player for whom shoes would eventually equal "financial security," remarked in his 1993 book *Shaq Attack!*, "It's funny, when I was just starting to play ball, kids didn't think much about shoes." Now they most certainly were. Every high school athlete worth his or her salt was already thinking shoe deal.

From Jordan on, the creation of a persona with strong, readily identifiable characteristics would be as important to the shoe companies as it was to the NBA. Since most basketball shoe consumers did not play basketball, the shoes clearly had an appeal beyond their functional attributes— a fact the shoe companies were slow to pick up on, but then pursued with abandon. Beyond simply emulating basketball stars, wearers of the shoes were becoming defined as part of a largely black, urban cutting-edge style that would eventually become essential to the sneaker industry. Where Adidas' rise in the early 1970s reflected a turn toward tennis-inflected "active wear" in American society, basketball dominated the new style, with high-top shoes and licensed jerseys showing up on—and, more importantly, off—the court. African American youth in the largest urban markets became the foot soldiers for a sneaker's success in mostly white suburban and rural areas, the eventual source of most of the profit (as Nike itself estimated in 1991, about 87 percent of its products were purchased by whites).

In the ascendant hip-hop culture of the 1980s, the sneaker was as signature a fashion accessory as L.L. Cool J's Kangol cap or Flavor Flav's oversized watch; and by the early 1980s it was not uncommon to see breakdancers wearing the suede Puma "Clyde" (the version, they claimed, made in the original Yugoslavian factory). The hip-hop "kicks" fetish reached its

Reebok
1996 sales: $2,360,000,000

Although best known in the United States for its white wrinkled-leather "Classic" aerobic shoe, Reebok dates to 1900, when track enthusiast Joseph William Foster began making running shoes in Bolton, England. Over the succeeding decade "Foster's boots" were donned by myriad Olympic athletes and English football clubs, such as Liverpool and Manchester United. Reebok's CEO, Paul Fireman, dropped out of college in 1979, to head his family's sporting goods business; among his initial moves he acquired the U.S. rights to three Reebok shoes (then emblazoned with the Union Jack). A production mishap produced the wrinkled-leather of its aerobic shoe, which became so popular it helped Reebok vault past Nike into first place in the United States and the company's revenues pushed from $13 million in 1983 to $1.4 billion in 1987. In 1984, Fireman bought out the parent company and acquired smaller companies, such as Ellesse and

Avia. In the 1990s, Reebok slipped to number two as it failed to match Nike's product output and advertising, and the mercurial Fireman was promoting EST sessions to boost workforce morale. In 1996, the Stoughton, Massachusetts-based Reebok signed a deal to distribute Ralph Lauren footwear, while continuing to enjoy success with basketball shoes endorsed by Shaquille O'Neal and Allen Iverson. The company has been recognized by the U.S. Department of Labor for its anti-sweatshop efforts and since 1992 has awarded an annual human rights prize, although it produces over 30 percent of its shoes in China, a country widely criticized for human rights abuses.

pinnacle in 1986 with the release of the song "My Adidas" by the rap trio Run-D.M.C., who set the trend of wearing laceless sneakers. Adidas, which had lost ground to Nike in the athletic arena in the 1980s, saw in the group a chance to cultivate new audiences. Run-D.M.C. joined the ranks of the athlete endorsers by eventually signing a sponsorship deal with the company.

Arcane shoe references abounded in the lyrics of performers, and the way one wore one's sneakers took on a symbolic cast, but the relationship ran deeper. Rappers such as Heavy D took to wearing tracksuits by Fila, the Italian fashion company known previously for equipping the strawberries-and-cream set. Fila was an early "aspirational brand;" in other words, buying it would indicate—or at least demonstrate an affinity to—a certain socioeconomic standing or lifestyle, in this case country-club casual (brands such as Nautica and Tommy Hilfiger would come later). In a market where the other traditional symbols of suburban affluence were scarce, sneakers bore a lot of weight. As a Newark, New Jersey shoe retailer told *Sports Illustrated* about his customers, "They buy shoes just like other Americans buy fancy cars and new suits. It's all about trying to find some status in the world." In Spike Lee's 1989 film, *Do the Right Thing*, the strident Buggin' Out responds vehemently to the ultimate affront—the scuffing of his new Air Jordans by a white, Larry Bird-jersey-wearing neighbor—and is later shown fastidiously cleaning them with a toothbrush.

Fila and other companies responded to their hip-hop cachet by methodically cultivating the "urban" market (in industry parlance, a code word for "black"). Fila's commercials, for example, were described by their advertising agency in *Forbes* as "edgy, dark, a little threatening"—spots replete with graffiti-tagged playgrounds and intimidating audio overlays. It was a thin line to walk, for the mainstream press was reporting that sneakers were drug dealers' fashion of choice, that gangs such as L.A.'s Crips and Bloods were buying shoes that matched their gang colors (and that company reps even sought them out to make the sale), and that drug dealers often paid their "runners" in new sneakers. In cities, the appearance of a pair of sneakers hanging over a street light or telephone line reportedly signaled the presence of dealers. As the culture critic Michael Eric Dyson wrote, "the sneaker reflects at once the projection and styliza-tion of black urban realities linked in our contem-porary historical moment to rap culture and the underground political economy of crack, and reigns as the universal icon for the culture of con-sumption." For Dyson, the sneaker also symbolized "the ingenious manner in which black cultural nuances of cool, hip, and chic have influenced the broader American cultural landscape."

Vans

1996 sales: $117,400,000

A shoe company based in Orange County, California, Vans' eponymous product vies with Airwalk, D.C., and lesser-known brands as the footwear of choice for skateboard-ers, snowboarders, mountain bikers, and style-conscious urbanites. Founded by Paul Van Doren and three other partners in 1966, Vans manufactured a vulcanized, gum rubber–soled shoe that proved more durable than Keds or Converse. First embraced by surfers, by the 1970s the shoes were a southern California staple. In 1982, Vans' popularity soared when Sean Penn's character Jeff Spicoli wore a check-ered pair in *Fast Times at Ridgemont High*. In the 1990s, after several years in and out of bankruptcy, Vans mounted a comeback. The company followed Nike's example and shut its California factory, moving most production to South Korea, where it could roll out new production lines more quickly (as well as manufacture its shoes using a solvent that is illegal in the United States). Vans solidified its core surf/skate lifestyle market (sponsoring the alt-rock Warped Tour) and spun off fashion-inspired releases such as the "Blunt," sold exclusively at the Manhattan boutique Patricia Fields. Vans' profits more than tripled from 1995 to 1996, and in 1997 the company launched a $25 million "Team Vans" marketing blitz, peppered with skating and surfing personalities and featuring commercials shot by *Kids* director Larry Clark.

As companies targeted the "urban" market, however, they were also reaching out to certain segments of the suburban market that, in a twist on the aspirational brand theory, often emulated the tough, urban culture beamed via satellite to the most pastoral settings. For the shoe companies, it was a tightrope. As an Avia salesman told the *Wall Street Journal* in 1988, "the inner city is a lucrative market

An Interview with Run-D.M.C.

How did it get started between Run-D.M.C. and Adidas?

D.M.C.: Growing up in Hollis, Queens, New York, everybody was wearing Pumas, everybody was wearing Nikes, and when we put on our Adidas we said we was never gonna take 'em off. And as things went on, down the line, you know, where D.M.C. was always representing with the Shelltoes, we made a record about it. Everybody was loving the record, and boom bang, and then Adidas, the company began to hear about it.

JMJ: Through our management, we met this guy named Tony, he was from Adidas. And he just came to the Garden.

D.M.C.: Run said, "If you got Adidas on, hold 'em up in the air." And thirty thousand people in Madison Square Garden held 'em up. They looked at that and said, "Y'all got a deal."

JMJ: He left there and gave us a promise. "If you don't get a deal, man, I'mma quit this company for good." You know what I'm saying?

Why didn't Adidas wanna work with you before that?

JMJ: I guess they didn't know what it was. All they knew was they were selling sneakers. And what it was, everywhere we were going, you couldn't buy Adidas in that town—no parts. No hats, no shirts, nothing. Anything that said Adidas that year was out of the stores. We'd do in-stores [in-store appearances] in malls and sporting stores, and everybody was buying Adidas.

and many trends start there, but 'inner-city' as a word is the kiss of death." To put it another way, the shoes had to be "black," but not "too black." Race was just another style available for consumption, but it was used selectively. Sneaker commercials carved out enduring representations of black athletes: the menacing embodiment of hard-edged street credibility, hulking performers of super-heroically charged exploits, or cartoonish cross-dressing jesters. Amid all the cross-marketing and media hype over the shoe's pernicious

You would do that stuff through Adidas?

JMJ: Naa, Adidas didn't have nothing to do with it. It would be the sporting goods guy's calling our management, "Yo, I need you to come down, man. We're gonna hook up with the record store man and they come through with a record man and I can sell a piece of Adidas." It was just hot.

So you were selling a lot of Adidas stuff before you were involved with them?

JMJ: We weren't even looking at it like that. We didn't make the song to be down with 'em, so we didn't care. We made the song 'cause I think Reebok was getting hot. And we wasn't feeling that at all. A couple of kids is running up on us, like "Why y'all don't get some Reebok?"

The same question was asked to all of us. Run and them, we gonna [begins scribbling lyrics] and they just came up with it. Me and Run put the beat down, and him and D did what they had to do.

And how long after the song came out that the shoes came out. It was like a year, wasn't it?

JMJ: To tell the truth, I never really felt those shoes... we didn't design those shoes. We had hot designs. Designs that D.M.C. made back then, they put out years later.

Did you guys ever go to any of the factories?

JMJ: We went to the original factory, where they made the first ones.

In Germany?

effects on inner-city neighborhoods, the sneaker was acquiring a sort of racial and class coding even as its popularity extended across a wide swatch of the American public. In Tom Wolfe's 1987 novel *The Bonfire of the Vanities*, which is, if nothing else, a document of how the mainstream viewed the Reagan-era metropolis, sneakers are hot-button badges of social disorder and identity-creating tokens. A crotchety Bronx judge, seeing the assistant district attorney clad in running shoes, growls: "Christ, every kid who sticks up a Red Apple's in my courtroom wearing those goddamn things, and now you guys?" A few pages earlier, the assistant district attorney rides a subway car that is rife with metaphorical footwear (*see next page*):

JMJ: Yeah, where they still got like, twenty people that's just doin' it. There's still OLD ladies doing them like this [makes hand stitching motion]. Where you can still get your original joints.

D.M.C.: We seen this Olympic history stuff. Saw a size fifteen Adidas for Bob Lanier. Seen all types of Olympic and Bill Cosby stuff. Everything.

What do you think of all the Old School stuff coming back, again?

D.M.C.: I think it's dope because right now, it seems all the sneaker companies are trying to outdo each other with all these wild designs and high-tech, futuristic stuff, and you look at the older styles and remember how comfortable they were, and how dope they looked.

JMJ: I always kept a closet full of Shells. And every time you bust a pair out, everybody'd be like "Oohhh." But some towns, like Boston, they never went nowhere.

Right.

JMJ: (smiling) I guess you can't really do this without going to Boston (laughs). Are you going to Boston?

No, but I hear that's true...

JMJ: Boston is the only city in America where they was three stripes... put it this way, like if you walk down the block with a pair of Nike's or something, down the wrong block on the wrong night, with some drunk people... you'd get stomped OUT. You can come with any kinda flavored three stripes through those ghettoes out there.

On the subway, the D train, heading for the Bronx, Kramer stood in the aisle, holding on to a stainless-steel pole while the car bucked and lurched and screamed. On the plastic bench across from him sat a bony old man who seemed to be growing like a fungus out of a backdrop of graffiti. He was reading a newspaper. The headline on the newspaper said HARLEM MOB CHASES MAYOR. The words were so big, they took up the entire page. Up above, in smaller letters, it said, "Go Back Down to Hymietown!" The old man was wearing a pair of purple-and-white striped running sneakers. They looked weird

37

You come with some other kind of sneakers, for real, they'll pick on you. When we went out there with Timberland's on, they were like, "Wassup wit da three stripes!? YO!" [Laughter.] Something about Roxbury, Boston. I don't know. They felt what we felt, but it's forever. They just vibing like that. We came back, Adidas really started coming back a couple years ago, I mean, really gettin' cool. 'Cause it got frustrating to us, because we were 100 percent down, more down. We ain't gettin' paid, we just want you to be HOT, stay hot. They didn't let us fight for 'em.

How did you guys get paid by Adidas? Was it per shoe?

JMJ: Yeah, we just got hit off. I don't even remember if it was a per-shoe thing. I know we just got a few check, over a million dollars. It was a million-dollar deal.

That's good.

D.M.C.: They gave us a lot of tour support. A LOT of tour support. And we're really thankful for that. They helped us out with a lot of charity stuff. And they sent us crazy stuff, like one tour we got so much still we was giving stuff away to Whodini and L.L. [Cool J.]... the cook, and workers, and policeman. I mean, we was handing out so much Adidas stuff.

JMJ: They looked out for us. I mean, I'm still looked out for. My kids are looked out for, my wife is looked out for.

on such an old man, but there was nothing really odd about them, not on the D train. Kramer scanned the floor. Half the people in the car were wearing sneakers with splashy designs on them and molded soles that looked like gravy boats. Young people were wearing them, old men were wearing them, mothers with children on their laps were wearing them, and for that matter, the children were wearing them. This was not for reasons of Young Fit & Firm Chic, the way it was downtown, where you saw a lot of well-dressed young white people going off to work in the morning wearing these sneakers. No, on the D train the reason was, they were cheap. On the D train these sneakers were like a sign around the neck reading SLUM or EL BARRIO.

Kramer resisted admitting to himself why he wore them.

What are some of your favorite products?

JMJ: I think the Shelltoes, you can't get around 'em. To me, that's like a pair of shoes, on a day when you can get geared up and just look NEAT. A clean pair of Shelltoes will always do it for you. HI-tops. The lo-top joints were the original ones, but I grew into the hi-tops. They just fit the jeans better. I don't know on the gear side.

D.M.C.: Yeah, I'm not sure of the number, I think it was the A-15 model... Yeah, the warm-ups.

JMJ: Anything they got with zippers on the pants. You gotta have a zipper on your pants.

—interview by Dan Field in Grand Royal #3 *(1996)*

BY THE END OF THE DECADE, the fervent urban marketing efforts of the shoe companies was to backfire. A few years earlier, the "shoe wars" was a journalist's favorite phrase to describe the battle between Nike and Reebok for market supremacy, but by 1990 that phrase meant something else entirely. That year, a rash of newspaper stories documented cases of young, urban, usually black males killing each other over sneakers (the pair most often cited was Nike's hundred-dollar-plus Air Jordans) and other branded apparel. "It's gotta be the shoes," the refrain of Spike Lee's "Mars Blackmon" spots for Nike, became shorthand for explaining a rash of drug-related muggings and killings. As *Sports Illustrated* put it in a widely discussed article, the shoe companies were "accused of creating a fantasy-fueled market for luxury items in the economically blasted inner cities and willingly tapping into the flow of drug and gang money." Suddenly, an ad that showed basketball player Michael Johnson holding a machine gun for L.A. Gear seemed even more wildly inappropriate, as did shoes such as Converse's "Weapons" or the "Run N' Gun." In Chicago, the Rev. Jesse Jackson criticized the companies for "exploiting an ethos of mindless materialism," and in September, announced an Operation PUSH–led boycott of Nike. Spike Lee, who two years earlier had brought the issue to the attention of Nike, was accused by the *New York Post* of "sellin' out" the black community by producing commercials for a maker of "ripoff shoes." Lee retorted, "Let's try to effectively deal with the conditions that make a kid put so much importance on a pair of sneakers, a jacket, and gold." Michael Jordan tried to sidestep the issue, just as he would a

Other Companies

There are literally dozens of other companies in the business of making athletic shoes, from sporting goods giant Spalding ($156 million in sales in 1996) to Ryka ($10.2 million in sales in 1996). However, the nearly twenty companies—excluding Reebok—ranked below Nike in total sales sold less combined than did Nike alone.

ASICS Tiger Corporation (the name ASICS is an acronym for the Latin phrase "Anima Sana In Corpore Sano," or, "A Sound Mind in a Sound Body") was founded in 1964 as Onitsuka Tiger by Kihachiro Onitsuka. The Japanese entrepreneur had an early distribution relationship with Phil Knight, until the latter broke away to form Nike. Although ranked ninth in sales in the U.S., ASICS—based in Japan—is a $2.5 billion company worldwide.

L.A. Gear, founded by a shopping mall developed in the early 1980s, exploded as a fashionable alternative to Reebok and Nike, doing especially well among women and in aerobics. While still ranked in the top ten in *sales in 1996, L.A. Gear has in recent years defaulted on debts and has had its stock removed from NASDAQ trading. California-based K-Swiss is a favorite among women and in tennis players and fans (with $76 million in sales in 1996); Ryka, Kaepa, and Avia have similar niches. British Knights, a big player in the basketball/hip-hop world in the 1980s (and reputedly a shoe of choice for gang members, who dubbed the shoe "brotha killers") and a sort of male equivalent of the fashionable L.A. Gear, is still licensed in the U.S. pulling in $60 million in sales in 1996, but has lost most of its influence. Karl Kani's line of sneakers—which, like the rest of the designer's oeuvre, prominently features his name—has done well among African American consumers, with some $20.8 million in sales in 1996.*

The Saucony Shoe Manufacturing Co., a Massachusetts-based running shoe company, was purchased by Hyde Athletic Industries (which also produces Spot-Bilt team athletic shoes)

few years later when pressed about the labor practices of Nike's Asian subcontractors.

There was a "sneaker madness" sensationalism to much of the coverage, which came from a media not known for being particularly attuned to the condition of poor, young urban minorities. Some of the outrage stemmed from seeing sneakers, a symbol of youthful innocence, turned into a motive for crime; indeed, when tragedy befalls a child, the sneaker is invoked with surprising frequency, to lend poignancy. In the case of a 1997 killing in New Jersey of an eleven-year-old boy by a fifteen-year-old boy, press accounts were careful to note that the victim had a "sneaker mark" on his back. Nirvana's lead singer, Kurt Cobain, an adult with an adolescent following, shot himself while wearing Converse Chuck Taylors. In the Stephen King short story "The Body," the terror involved in discovering a child killed by a train is driven home by seeing the boy's tennis shoes lying askance the body: "The train had knocked him out of his Keds just as it had knocked the life out of his body."

Yet in the "shoe wars" coverage there was also an implicit critique of the marketing of increasingly expensive shoes to the poor—a rare questioning of the decade's intensification of consumerism and commercialism.

It was, however, conspicuously limited to black consumers. The *U.S. News & World Report* columnist John Leo told the *New York Times* in 1990 that the "Just Do It" campaign took on a special meaning when applied to lower-income areas: "To the middle class, it means get in shape, whereas in the ghetto it means, 'Don't have any moral compunction—just go out and do whatever you have to do in your predicament.' There's an immoral message in there." Leo chose to ignore the larger moral backdrop of the 1980s: speculative greed on Wall Street, deep social spending cuts, a dramatic rise in personal consumer debt, and a popular culture that shamelessly extolled the virtues of the sybaritic life. He also ignored the question of what appeal the edgy, inner-city ads might have to consumers who did not live in such areas. Athletic shoes were as much a "lifestyle" product for black urban youth as they were for affluent white suburbanites, but somehow it was qualitatively better when the latter group wore them—even as they enjoyed commercials set in the inner-city. That sneakers should be at the center of a national debate, charged with the same moral consequences as out-of-wedlock children or drug dealing, was yet further testimony to their transformation from recreational equipment to social symbol, multibillion-dollar business, and way of life.

in 1968. It has a strong market niche in women's running; its shoes are produced in Bangor, Maine. Etonic is another Massachusetts-based athletic shoe company with deep roots in the area—Charles Eaton began making shoes in 1867. A niche player in the running category, Etonic was purchased first by Colgate-Palmolive in 1975 and then by the Swedish athletic shoe company Tretorn (now down to annual sales of $7 million in the U.S.) and then finally by Spalding. Brooks is another company that comes out of the New England shoemaking tradition, and in the 1970s it battled Nike for supremacy in the running shoe market. It has been in and out of financial difficulty, although under the leadership of ex-Nike employee Helen Rockey, Brooks—owned by The Rokke Group, a Norwegian concern— has returned to profitability. Several sporting goods companies make their own line of branded sneakers. Spalding is the U.S.'s longest-running manufacturer of sporting goods and produces a range of tennis and other shoes, popular in sporting good and department stores. The Japanese sporting goods giant Mizuno Corporation (a $2 billion global concern) is dominant in baseball shoes; New Jersey-based Prince has seen its tennis shoes increase in popularity (the company sold $10 million worth in 1996), although it still lags tennis-equipment giant Wilson at $18.5 million. Florida-based Ellesse ($7 million in sales in 1996), owned by the British conglomerate Pentland Group PLC (which owns Speedo and a number of other brands and backed off buying Adidas in 1992), is popular among the younger tennis-playing set, but has been plagued by declining sales.

A number of foreign athletic shoe makers have a small presence here in such niche areas as soccer and volleyball. Italian firms Lotto, Umbro, and Diadora (another athletic shoe company that got its start during World War II, when Marcello Danielli began making

42

How a Shoe Became a Lifestyle

BY THE 1990S, the shoe companies had become fashion and marketing giants. They were also rewriting the rules of sports, and nowhere was this more true than in basketball. "I work for Nike," the NBA rookie Alonzo Mourning baldly admitted. While at the 1992 Olympics in Barcelona, the irrepressible Nike-endorser Charles Barkley pithily noted that "he had two million reasons not to wear Reebok," which was the equipment sponsor for the U.S. Olympic basketball team. Under Commissioner David Stern, the NBA had taken a superstar, personality-driven approach to marketing the league, turning a handful of basketball players essentially into tennis stars. The NBA became a brand, something bigger than the game itself; sales of its licensed merchandise, as a consequence, rose from $10 million in 1982 to $2.5 billion by 1995. As a Reebok executive put it, "The NBA was the first to industrialize the entertainment aspect of it all. The glamour and glitz. The music in the arenas. Everything. It's about entertainment, and they've done it well."

Basketball was also a sport that needed little equipment, save shoes, and it allowed its fans the closest look at the players' faces—and feet. As basketball shoes eclipsed running shoes as the most popular style (they now account for roughly a quarter of the market), the endorsement culture reached a fever pitch. In 1995, Michael Jordan, Grant Hill, and Shaquille O'Neal were each, by all reliable accounts, making more in shoe revenue than all NBA players combined had received for shoe deals during any year in the 1970s—and possibly the entire decade. While shoe deals were becoming more grandiose, the bulk of the money was going to a few top players, with most other players getting very small deals. As each company focused on one or two players per sport, a small number of NBA rookies (including Stephon Marbury and Samaki Walker) looking to not get lost in the marketing shadows, began signing endorsement deals with smaller companies—Apex One, AND 1, Balls N, and so on—that previously had not made sneakers.

The shoe industry itself, like the endorsement structure, was becoming emblematic of what Robert Frank and Thomas Cook have called the "winner-take-all society," in which extreme disparity characterizes compensation in various markets. After a decade of intense advertising and design innovation, Nike had captured over 40 percent of the market and, paired with Reebok, controlled more than half. Nike is estimated to have spent $643 million marketing its shoes in 1996, compared with $42 million by then-number-five Converse. Still, a campaign based

boots for the Italian army), as well as Major League Soccer-endorser Mitre are trying to fight off Nike's penetration into soccer. France's Patrick has a very small U.S. presence, also primarily in soccer.

And then there's Skechers and Simple, California-based companies that like Airwalk and Vans have carved out sizable niches in the "casual sneaker" category (the two companies, which sell other types of shoes as well, had 1996 sales of $134 million and $26.2 million). Many fondly remember Pony, a leading basketball and wrestling shoe in the 1970s; like Ellesse, it is owned by Pentland and is still in operation. Finally, a whole host of small footwear vendors such as Power, Xanthus, Turntec, and U.S. Athletic battle with off-brand shoes and brand-name close-outs at the lower end of the price-point spectrum.

around one player and one shoe could lift a company out of the crowded pack: Grant Hill helped Fila rocket into third place, while a Dr. J commemorative shoe helped Converse more than double its sales in a year. The importance of a shoe deal with dramatized in the 1996 film *Jerry Maguire*, in which the wide receiver Rod "Show Me the Money" Tidwell chastises Reebok for overlooking him. Yet an inadvertent twist revealed another force in the sneaker industry: product placement. Reebok sued Tri-Star Pictures for dropping a scene—a mock Tidwell commercial for Reebok that was shot and paid for by the shoe company—from the final cut: after an out-of-court settlement was reached, a cable version of the film featured a 47-second mock Reebok commercial. Nike did better with the Cortez-clad Forrest Gump. When the eponymous film was released, *Advertising Age* noted that it was providing "image enhancement for the Nike brand." (The company was not so lucky when the members of southern California's Heaven's Gate cult were all found dead in matching black Nikes in the summer of 1997, an episode satirized on *Saturday Night Live*, among other venues.)

"We live in a world where consumer products can define, or at least be outward badges, of a person's character," a Reebok marketing official told the *New York Times*. Somewhere along the line in their mercurial history, sneakers had gone from "once lowly" part-time shoes to "badges" of character; whether they were retro Puma Clydes on the feet of a cutting-edge rock musician or politically useful "Made in the U.S.A." New Balance on President Clinton (before he jumped on the free-trade "fast track," at least). The range of styles and models had expanded to the point where it seemed no activity was without a shoe—walking, a new market category, was third behind basketball and cross-training.

Nike, which had about fifty styles of shoe in 1977, had over three hundred a decade later. Sneakers were the perfect accessory for a new global style of casual clothing that blended utility with fashion, emphasized speed and mobility, stressed disposability and change rather than permanence. The market's capaciousness could comfortably accommodate both the dominant Nike, which prided itself on its technical roots, and a host of "anti-Nike" niche companies, such as Airwalk, Simple, and Vans, which sold low-tech shoes—originally the stuff of skateboarders

45

FIGURE 4   *Total U.S. Footwear Market, 1996*

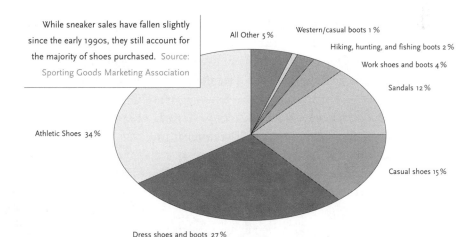

While sneaker sales have fallen slightly since the early 1990s, they still account for the majority of shoes purchased. Source: Sporting Goods Marketing Association

All Other 5%

Western/casual boots 1%

Hiking, hunting, and fishing boots 2%

Work shoes and boots 4%

Sandals 12%

Casual shoes 15%

Athletic Shoes 34%

Dress shoes and boots 27%

and others—to a new lifestyle-driven market that fully reached the mainstream in the 1990s. "Vans is all about lifestyle," the company's CEO said in 1996, while the company report dwelled more on brand than on product: "The VANS brand image coincides with what the company believes is a fundamental shift in the attitude and lifestyles of young people worldwide, characterized by the rapid growth and acceptance of the alternative, outdoor sports and the desire to lead an individualistic, contemporary lifestyle." Sneakers were part of a contemporaneous cut-and-paste vocabulary of media-transmitted global hip, a phenomenon seized upon by Airwalk president Lee Smith: "If they want to be the geek-nerd girl in Japan, it's the same as the geek-nerd girl in New York."

In both Tokyo and New York, meanwhile, vintage Nike Cortez and Adidas Gazelle "vintage" meaning from the 1970s and 1980s) were selling for upward of five hundred dollars a pair. Echoing an earlier U.S. phenomenon, Japanese children were reportedly being robbed for their new Nike Air Max's, which were selling at five times their suggested retail price, according to *Asiaweek*. Venerable shoes such as Keds and Chuck Taylors had survived the cultural revolution through carefully wrought nostalgia and back-to-basics campaigns. The sneaker, which technology and fashion had threatened to make obsolete, had come back—but as what? In the late 1980s, Stride-Rite trained focus groups on Keds, asking, "If Keds were a building, what kind of building would it be?" The usual answer was "a country house with a white picket fence" (Nike was a glass office building). Pro-Keds, discontinued in 1984, brought back a canvas sneaker, while P.F. Flyers were reintroduced as a carefully positioned branded product for Baby Boomers, with in-store displays evoking those same warm childhood memories embodied by the shoe itself. "We're positioning this as the sneaker of the twenty-first century," a P.F. Flyers executive told *Footwear News* in 1991, which meant timeless styling but a higher price; shortly afterward, however, the shoe was repositioned again as a moderately priced canvas sneaker sold in mass-market department stores. Memories are only worth so much.

By the 1990s, the "traditional" approach still worked, but as often as not the shoes were upgraded with a thick slab of "rave" sole or tinted a searing fuschia, as fashion designers such as Todd Oldham were brought on board to put their stamp on the blank white canvas. Fashion companies such as Tommy Hilfiger and DKNY were getting into the sneaker market, while Oldham was designing Keds. As the sneaker century drew to a close, fin-de-siècle footwear was in a Janus phase, looking ahead to the next breakthrough material and looking back to the material memories of a simpler age.

2

The Game Plan

Design and Implementation

"I can't imagine what the shoes would look like
in ten years if they went at this rate."
—Brooks marketing employee

Windows to the Sole

IN THE 1961 DISNEY FILM *The Absent-Minded Professor*,
Fred MacMurray plays a high school basketball coach who
invents flubber: a miracle "flying rubber" for shoes that trans-
forms his also-rans into champions. In 1997, the film was
remade starring Robin Williams, and the quest for flubber was
still a viable story thread. Since the days of the Dassler brothers'
foot race, shoe companies have been searching for a technological
breakthrough that would give their shoe a perceptible edge over its
competitors. In recent years, the design curve has peaked so high that,
as a Brooks marketing employee remarked, "I can't imagine what the
shoes would look like in ten years if they went at this rate." Another
designer insists it has only begun, suggesting that lighter-than-air
elements like helium may one day inhabit our shoes. In light of the
tectonic shifts in shoe design over the past few decades, the fact that the
NBA's Larry Bird actually played in Converse Chuck Taylors into the late
1970s seems almost as farfetched as the thought of
A. J. Foyt racing the Indy 500 at the same time in a Ford Model-T.

One result of this convulsive innovation is that sneakers are subject to a
twin form of planned obsolescence: if they do not go out of style first, the
technology will be eclipsed by the next-generation pad or pod, cell or gel. Like
Detroit on amphetamines, sneaker makers roll out on average four new lines a
year, each batch loaded with new colors, styles, and technology features—all of which
are often replaced by the following year. "We used to have two seasons, but it's more
like four now," Fila's Bob Liewald told the *Dallas Morning News*. "We have to recreate

ourselves every ninety days with new product in each category—cross-training, running, tennis. We have to bring out the new." In a crowded market where distinguishing features are scant, design, like advertising, has become crucial for making a shoe stand out on the shelf and in the consumer's mind.

Sneaker designers, who usually come to their profession through some vaguely associated field (for example, architecture or movie set design), have become celebrities of sorts: Nike's Tinker Hatfield has been the subject of numerous magazine profiles and was named by the design magazine *ID* as one of the top designers on the West Coast; Reebok's Spencer White, meanwhile, was shown in 1997 company ads asking runners to stop and sample DMX, the company's next-wave cushioning system, while his figure appeared on cardboard cutouts in the nation's stores. Inspiration for athletic shoe design is drawn from myriad industrial and pop cultural sources, from the P-51 Mustang fighter plane to NASA to graffiti to the high-tech Denver airport, while designers consort with biomechanical engineers to match shoe design to the optimum performance of the human foot. (In publications such as the *American Journal of Sports Medicine*, one can read about the "maximal voluntary resistances to inversion moments" when an athlete is wearing a high-top shoe.) Nike, for one, has doubled its design staff and tripled its research and development budget since 1995, and according to officials at a 1997 analyst's meeting, is planning "a relentless flow of new product technologies and designs," including "Skysole" and "visible zoom-air." Nike employs over three hundred designers, while Reebok has roughly sixty on staff and Fila, forty. Statistics routinely claim that roughly 80 percent of athletic-shoe wearers will not use them for any kind of sporting pursuit. Still, sneaker companies strive to have top athletes as their standard-bearers and work to develop technologies that sound reasonably advanced, yet make sense to the consumer. Whatever edge is gained is purely in the realm of perception; as a 1997 Salomon Brothers industry report put it, "No company has publicized that its cushioning system outperforms another because generally these cushioning technologies perform no better than regular polyurethane (PU) or ethylene-vinyl acetate (EVA) foam. Investing in the creation and strong marketing of these technologies provides a credibility to companies that their product will actually help with true athletic performance, and thus help give a specific brand an aura of being an authentic athletic brand." The image of athletic integrity can imbue an entire line with a positive aura; a "fashion" perception, meanwhile, can spark a trend or draw new customers, but is perceived as risky in the long term. The "technology" companies routinely introduce innovations in high-end performance shoes, and as labor and materials costs go down the features spread to the "mid-pricepoint" region. The design, in theory, flows from the athletic core outward, although fashion is never absent from the design process of even the most advanced athletic shoes. The writer Randy Gragg, in a piece on Nike, describes how the company relies on a symbiosis of intensely focused, fine-grained technical improvements and timely doses of mythic human performance to put its product—in this case the gold-plated cleats of sprinter Michael Johnson—forward:

Few examples illustrate the process so elegantly as 200-meter sprinter Michael Johnson's record-shattering performance in the 1996 Olympics, which was further gilded by the color of his shoes. As much as a fashion statement or an expression of athletic hubris, Johnson's 14-carat cleats were a radical and carefully technical design innovation.

Two years before the Olympics, according to Michael Donaghu, head of Nike's Advanced Products Engineering Group (the in-house 10-engineer, 10-designer R&D wing), the company began looking for areas in equipment design in which it might make significant advancements, finally seizing upon the sprint, and, with surgical specificity, focusing on one aspect of the 200-meter dash. "We realized running the corner had never been considered," Donaghu says. "That's when we interjected Michael [Johnson] into the process. He's a committed athlete who is particular about his needs. Most people who get to that level are in tune with every piece that constitutes progress."

Donaghu, a former competitive athlete (a long-distance runner at Dartmouth) like so many Nike employees, explains the basic design problem was to turn angular momentum into straight line energy— an equation that is both physical and psychological. Instead of the mesh overlays typically used for breathability, the designers used a thin, metallic fabric for a glove-like fit as well as for its real and visually per-ceived aerodynamism. Instead of replaceable, and therefore heavier, conical-shape metal cleats, Johnson ran on permanent ones. Made from a lighter ceramic-and-aluminum metal matrix, they were molded into a telescoping series of concentric rings that grip without any drag-inducing puncture of the track's surface. Perhaps most important, unlike any previous sprinter's shoes, Johnson's were asymmetrical. The turn in the 200-meter dash is always left. Consequently, Nike's designers added a plastic, claw-like cleat to the inside of the right shoe and to the outside of the left, allowing for better traction in the angle of the turn.

At just over three ounces, the shoe weighed barely half as much as the previous world-class product with which Johnson had won the world championship two years before. The final gold plating of the shoes was, according to Donaghu, Johnson's suggestion, a "dare to himself," the risk being the fashion disaster of having to wear a medal that didn't match. Surface ostentation notwithstanding, the shoe, according to Donaghu, "was an exercise in minimalism through the eyes of someone running the corner of a track faster than anybody ever has."

Though few product development scenarios have been so pure as the one that culminated in Johnson's gold-plated victory, Nike's consistency in divining the drama of sports at the moment of maximum marketing is unmatched. Think of the debut of the "Bo Knows" ad campaign in the 1989 baseball All-Star game, when Bo Jackson, first time at bat, slammed a home run and went on to win the MVP award. Or think simply of Michael Jordan and his personal shoe designer Tinker Hatfield's thirteen versions of the Air Jordan.

FEW USERS WILL EVER push their shoes to the limits demanded by world-class sprinters, but design and technological innovations, as well as the faces of famous athletes, are essential to the sales pitch. As Nike's Philip Knight put it, "We've come around to saying that Nike is a marketing-oriented company, and the product is our most important marketing tool... [T]he design elements and functional characteristics of the product itself are just a part of the overall marketing process." Elaborate brochures and promotional videos typically accompany a new shoe on its release, and just as a car salesman has to be able to tell you what's under the hood, shoe salesmen at the retail chains are debriefed as to the competing technologies.

FIGURE 5 *Types of Athletic Shoes Sold in the U.S., 1996*

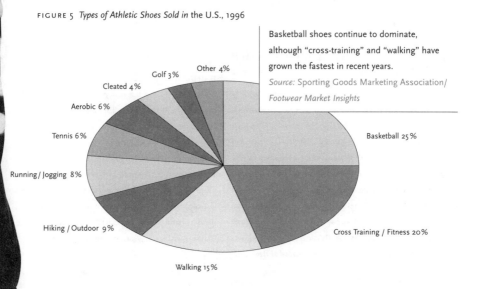

Basketball shoes continue to dominate, although "cross-training" and "walking" have grown the fastest in recent years.
Source: Sporting Goods Marketing Association/ *Footwear Market Insights*

Golf 3%
Other 4%
Cleated 4%
Aerobic 6%
Tennis 6%
Running/Jogging 8%
Hiking/Outdoor 9%
Basketball 25%
Cross Training/Fitness 20%
Walking 15%

"It's Not the Shoes," declared one ad for a health drink in 1997, the claim hovering over a sprinter ready to launch from the starting blocks. The shoe companies, however, have spent millions of dollars marketing—in industry parlance, "educating the consumer" about—the increasingly elaborate technologies of their respective products. It goes back to the 1950s, when P.F. Flyers promised to help boys "jump higher, run faster" and Adi Dassler touted a "vulcanized nylon sole without a leather middle layer" (while brother Rudi offered a "living nylon shoe with Air Conditioning"). It escalated in the United States in the early 1970s, after the track star Bill Bowerman, inspired by his waffle iron, designed the "waffle sole." In 1977, Nike developed "Air," or pockets of pressurized gas, which eventually became recognized as the industry's benchmark cushioning and the first to capture the

An Interview with Gordon Thompson III of Nike

No company has crafted a more coherent and widely recognized image than Nike. As part of a conscious effort to meld its products, corporate ethos, and an athletic-entertainment-fueled brand equity, Nike has expanded its design and research and development divisions in the past few years. One of the key figures is Gordon Thompson III, vice president of research, design and development, a job that includes, according to a press release, "footwear and apparel design and product development and the image division (film and video, graphic design and environmental design)."

How long does it take to design a shoe?

It depends on the athlete who's going to wear it—who it's designed for. It takes more time if there is a lot of new technology, and it depends on how the shoe's going to be manufactured and put together. We've had shoes take all of three years—from concept to shelf. On average the design time of a shoe is about 6 months—that's design development to the sales meeting. Average design time, itself, is about three months. Then, it takes a year to commercialize the product.

consumer imagination. Since then, a veritable Silicon Valley frenzy has engulfed the athletic shoe industry, with periodic breakthroughs that presume to make one company's technology superior, or at least noticeably distinct, to Brand X or last year's model. Waffles are strictly breakfast fodder these days, as today's CAD-equipped designers conspire with chemical companies to produce new compounds, dabble in advanced biomechanics, and draw on composites once proprietary to the aerospace industry. As Reebok's Spencer White observed, "What's been interesting in this business in the last ten years is that there was a time when we were going out to the automobile industry, or the medical industry, and looking at what materials they use and how we can borrow them." In the last few years, he claims, "Some of those industries are now coming to us to find out how we're evolving technologies and materials."

What about ideas research and development?

In footwear design there's advanced product engineering that begins 1-3 years prior to the delivery date. We look to running, for example, in the future and decide what we need in terms of new fabrics, materials, cushioning systems and other new ideas. And then there's a group that works 3-7 years ahead of delivery date. It's made up of twelve people who get really abstract about the way things are going and how we're going to progress. Foot dimensions, smart product, customization—they consider all of those things.

Do you have any plans for computer chips in the shoes?

We've knocked that idea around a lot. I think someone will get there first—I don't know if it will be us. What a chip does for you, and what it tells you, is something of debatable value when you talk to an athlete. For the average runner, it would be great to know how far you ran, then you could get your average split time, your timing per mile or half-mile—chips could do all these things. It can get pretty complex. We think the technology is there to connect something you'd wear on your wrist to something you'd wear on your feet—it's just how to implement the idea—that's the problem. We've worked with Apple, Microsoft, and the Media Lab at MIT—we have an alliance with them and they're a great source of inspiration to us.

Shoes routinely feature windows to the sole: clear plastic views into what is driving the shoe, whether silicon, Carbon-Kevlar, or some trademarked composite, such as Duralon or Stytherm. Catalogs are supplemented with charts showing "maximum penetration" and "midsole deterioration" and companies make bold claims, promising athletic shoes that are "capable of anything" and "a shoe so advanced, it is instinctive in its reactions." But what shoe design essentially boils down to, aside from weight and durability, are the twin poles of cushioning and stability. To enhance one compromises the other, so each design walks a fine line: too much stability and the shoe may feel uncomfortable; too much cushioning and it may feel

You make a certain amount of decisions that have nothing to do with comfort or injury prevention but with style. Do these style decisions masquerade as technological innovations?

I think that's a matter of how you define innovation. We don't make gratuitous design decisions. If we're going to do an interesting lacing on a shoe, we'll make sure it works. It may be aesthetically pleasing, but it better work. When I discuss the fashion question I always say that when you're designing for Pete Sampras, Andre Agassi and Michael Jordan, they're not going to take crap and stick it on their foot. They wear the exact same product, so we're dealing with a pretty high level of product integrity.

How many shoes do you produce of a given model?

That depends on the shoe. A highly successful shoe like Air Max will be about 200,000 pairs in the U.S. and about 350,000 worldwide. That would be the initial run and then there would be color updates throughout the season. Often there are 2 or 3 colors for one shoe.

How many models are there at the moment?

Too many. [laughs] We design about 300 shoes a year. And, even worse, within worldwide footwear, apparel, and equipment there are between 10,000 and 11,000 projects a year. We're putting a lot out there.

Do you pay attention to fashion designers—like Comme Des Garçon and Yojhi Yamamoto?

Of course. The best designers always know what's going on in the world. We know what's going on in film, in sports, in fashion—where all of the trends are going.

may feel like you're running on a waterbed (some runners use the phrase "Nike knee" to refer to a condition that allegedly develops from running on too much cushioning). Adding to the confusion are disagreements over what serves an athlete better: to be closer to the ground and "feel" the playing surface, or to be safely elevated by a platform of bulging polyurethane foam. Finding real differences in design takes some work. Nike's Air and Reebok's DMX, for example, are distinguished mostly by the fact that the latter's air shifts between two chambers, while the former's does not; and that Nike uses pressurized air while Reebok goes with "ambient pressure" (or, in layman's terms, the air one breathes). Yet

Do we sit and ponder what Yojhi's going to come up with this season? No. I'll think of someone like Issey Miyake, partly because I think his product is amazingly engineered. I'll look at how he seams something together and what kind of materials he used. You can definitely take inspiration from something like that. But about what Ralph Lauren is sticking on Kate Moss—I don't give a shit.

Are there corporate spies?

Yes. We've been broken into a number of times. We've had stuff stolen from dumpsters. Now our design building has double security—you have to have a pass to get in. It's not a huge problem but it's something we're aware of because of the proximity of other companies. Adidas is located in Portland and Fila just opened a design studio in Portland. I'm sure it's no secret why Adidas stuck their headquarters in Portland when it used to be back East. It wasn't just because of the weather.

Can you improve upon the shoe lace?

The shoe lace is very difficult. Getting the right length, getting one that doesn't untie when you're running or playing hoop. We've had a lot of ideas about combining shoe laces with customization fit— like two different sets of laces to enable you to open up to the shoe—we've tried lacing on the side of the shoe—we're continually looking at the laces' location and how it can make the shoe fit better. And also how to stop it from untying when you're running.

Isn't the percentage of non-athletic people wearing Nike increasing?

The percentage may be increasing but I think that young people are increasingly athletic.

as in the computer industry, new technological developments are heralded as watershed moments. "The technology of midsoles has become a bit ho-hum," said Puma's president, Herb Elliot, in 1996, announcing the company's foamless, elastomer-based shoes. "This takes a quantum leap forward."

The proliferation of technology has even spawned a back-to-nature countermovement, led by Adidas' Peter Moore (an early Nike employee). The design concept, called "Feet You Wear," was rolled out with as much marketing as its high-tech counterparts and is based on the notion that the human foot is the best piece of running equipment ever made. "We know your foot works.

Yes, but rock bands are wearing the shoes. You don't design for the non-athlete?

Like rock bands? [laughs] No! Then we'd totally lose our focus. If we go down that road and athletes put on a pair of tennis shoes and severely injure themselves, we're hosed—we've totally blown the idea of our product.

Even the design of the non-performance aspects of the shoe?

I don't think we need to pull in some young punk who's customized his laces and suggest that we copy it. We should be leading—Nike is not about following. I wouldn't work for Nike if they began following.

Do you make more concessions to non-design departments than you would like?

I'm a designer, so of course I think the answer is yes. [laughs] Nike's a matrix organization—we're one of the few companies that are actually like that. Since we're set up in matrix there's a lot of dialogue and lots of communication. Concessions are not made solely by design. Instead of saying, "Design has to take $10 off the price of a shoe," it's more like, "let's take $5 off the design and $5 off the advertising." I think people in the company have a good sense of design and realize that design is what makes the product exciting, new and innovative. We imagine that once the world is a homogenous mall—when entertainment retail is everywhere—some interesting design will start to grow between the cracks. We call that Zip Code Design.

—from "Fast on His Feet," by Dike Blair and Elein Fleiss, Purple Prose #12 (1997).

We copied it," one ad ran. "Straps, pumps, air pockets and other perceived enhancements," said Moore in a company announcement, "actually prevent the foot from doing the one thing it does best: being a foot." Denouncing "high-tech bells and whistles," Moore attempted to take some air out of the competition. "Every time a manufacturer introduces a new technology, they try to come up with some name that makes it appear bigger than it really is." As striking as Moore's approach seemed amidst the blizzard of gadgetry, the notion of using the foot as blueprint is hardly new: an ASICS ad in the early 1970s, for example, reads, "The best training shoe is more like a foot than a shoe. We give your feet what nature didn't." This is a typical strategy of advertising: take something natural and claim to make it better.

The Selfish Swoosh

THE STRIPES AND OTHER MARKINGS on the sides of athletic shoes once served as patented support systems, but design improvements have rendered such touches obsolete. The three Adidas stripes and the Nike swoosh are, obviously, simply logos. For the sneaker makers, however, they are the coin of the realm in an age of acute brand consciousness, widespread licensing, and border-crossing logo appeal. Shoe design is subsumed by a larger strategy: an entire design scheme incorporating logo, athletes, and lifestyle. This has only intensified as branded apparel sales began to weigh heavier on companies' balance sheets; thus we see Adidas, for example, allowing Los Angeles fashion designer

Laura Whitcomb to produce dresses with Adidas-style stripes running down the side. No single logo matches Nike's swoosh for visibility, however, a global constant running from downtown billboards to the caps of migrant workers in the Third World. Designed on the cheap in the early 1970s by Caroline Davidson, a Eugene, Oregon, art student, there is nothing inexpensive or accidental about its present ubiquity. As the writer Phil Patton describes it, the swoosh is the kernel from which all Nike design flows, a "selfish meme" driving the design itself, an effort so successful it can now appear by itself:

from **"The Tyranny of the Swoosh,"** by Phil Patton,

in *AIGA Journal of Graphic Design* (1996):

At the mall, we walk into the athletic-shoe stores, marveling at how many there are—Athlete's Foot, Foot Locker, Take Me Out to the Ball Game, Herman's—and how many new models appear between our visits. My kids and I check out the latest arrivals rack: new carbon composite Nike Air basketball shoes, the new white patent leather Jordan. We regular mall marchers have noticed something else: how the Nike swoosh has more and more and more come to decorate products in the vast Nike line—floating all by itself, an icon, without the company name.

The swoosh has become one of the most powerful logos of our era. It ornaments—and here an epic catalog is required—not just shoes but caps, running suits, socks, scarves, headbands, and water bottles. It is set on ovals at the end of wire racks and embossed in leather jackets, printed in trompe l'oeil embroidery patterns on hang tags, upholstered in shiny white patent leather, marked out in mesh on warm-up suits, cut out of neoprene and raised in suede. Part of the effect is to produce flocks, schools, swarms of swooshes floating across displays of caps, of socks, of shirts.

At Nike Towns, the company's showcase stores cum museums ... the swoosh becomes a 3-D form, rendered in chromed steel as part of the stair and balcony rails designed by in-house architect and design whiz Gordon Thompson.... In one of Nike's television ads, featuring Dennis Hopper, the swoosh in the oval morphs into a bone in a steak, a clever video pun in the tradition of MTV and the Disney Channel on-air logos. And Swoosh is the title of a book recounting an insider's view of the rise of Nike.

The swoosh's liberation from letter and word began ... when Andre Agassi won the men's championship at Wimbledon. It happened like this, according to Ron Dumas of Nike. Nike had just signed up Jim Courier and designed a line of clothes that emphasized his Americanness by taking cues from baseball uniforms—stripes, and a cap that displayed just the Nike swoosh, like a Cleveland Indian or a Florida Marlin. But Agassi donned the same cap; when he won, his picture decorated, among other media venues, the front page of the *New York Times*.

The Name of the Game

Nike earned the enmity of Muslims in 1997, when it produced a shoe whose rear logo bore letters resembling the Arabic spelling of "Allah." Nike PR reps quickly issued an apology and canceled the shoe, thus avoiding a "Satanic Sneakers" footwear *fatwah*. Reebok invoked one of the devil's minions when it released a women's athletic shoe called the "Incubus"; luckily, it was so dubbed only on the box and not the shoe. Adidas, perhaps confirming the suspicions youth have always had of the trademark trefoil symbol's vague similarity to the marijuana leaf, ran into trouble with the DEA when it issued a "Hemp" shoe.

All these missteps speak to a time-honored truism of sneaker mythology: names make all the difference. From "Chuck Taylors" to "P.F. Flyers" to "Stan Smiths" to "Air Jordans," a good name is an invaluable tool in helping to build mystique and craft personality around what is otherwise a lifeless

63

hunk of synthetic byproducts. As one might expect, sneaker names are generally meant to connote better performance in athletics. Speed, aggressiveness, aerodynamism, technical precision, prowess, intimidation, ruggedness, and physics-controverting motions are the desired outcome. Thus names like "Attack" and "React," "Carom" and "Kaboom," "Flight" and "Lightning." Nike in particular thrives on movement, stringing together small zip words for effect, e.g., the Nike "Air Movin' Uptempo," the "Air Zoom Flight" (for rougher skies you may desire Nike's "Air Flight Turbulence.") Even the signature shoe has taken on sharper, streamlined monikers: from "Stan Smiths" and "Jack Purcells" to "The Stack" (for Jerry Stackhouse) and "Shaqnosis" (for Shaquille O'Neal).

The swoosh caps became popular and Nike designers and marketers saw the usefulness—as they tried to expand sales outside the U.S.—of a logo that transcended language. So the swoosh began to break free.

The swoosh-marked products that mall walkers encounter are part of a wide design transformation. Beginning with a top-level meeting in 1995. Dumas and other designers persuaded top Nike management to use the swoosh logo, sans the more familiar lettered name, as the keynote of a whole corporate image rehaul—a change in everything from hang tags to boxes to stationery and business cards. The old logo, with the Nike letters, says Dumas, seemed very eighties. It had a big, corporate feel to it. The swoosh, by contrast, has something pure to it. And, Dumas reports, recognition of the swoosh alone as Nike's symbol ranged above the ninetieth percentile in consumer surveys.

The swoosh may be the most widely visible icon in sports, and in the world of global marketing it joins a list of very few trademarks completely free of association with names or letters. Think for a moment and you will note how short the list is: McDonald's Golden Arches, although even here there is a visual pun on the 'M' of McDonald's, the Shell scallop, perhaps, and the bold Texaco star, or the Mercedes tri-star or the Chevrolet bowtie; the tortured hieroglyph associated with the artist formerly known as Prince; and, to smaller audiences, Apple's apple and Greyhound's dog (cleaned up by Raymond Loewy).

Evoking a checkmark and a boomerang, the swoosh may be unique in suggesting movement and sound. As one ad reads, "Swoosh is the sound you make blowing by somebody." Abstract and rather graceful, it is also an extremely versatile graphic element. But, ironically, one of the advantages of the swoosh by itself is that it goes well with other images.

The swoosh appears in cross-licensing deals almost as an imprimatur, like the Olympic rings. Nike's growth from running-shoe company to basketball-shoe company to sports giant has seen the swoosh come to cohabit with professional team logos, college mascots, and even Warner Brothers characters on sweatshirts and in ads. Like the checkmark it resembles—the swoosh, by the way, seems to come from a right hand, not a southpaw's, except when it rides the right side of a shoe—it serves as a stamp of approval from the organization *Sports Illustrated* once called the most powerful force in sports.

Just as with cars, animal names have always had a place among sneakers. Indeed, Puma, Pony, Cougar, and Reebok christened their companies after fauna (the last after a South African antelope-like creature). The Adidas "Gazelle," Puma "Beast," Converse "Piranha," and the brief novelty sensation of "Kangaroos" (which contained small pouches but alas were not, as was the industry standard in the 1950s, made from kangaroo leather) stand out here. Others steal from the souped-up stock car: the "Nitro" or the "Afterburner." The newest shoes—like the newest cars—use random, consultant-picked names that tend to be pleasing Greek derivatives (similar to the words picked for new pharmaceuticals) or short, fizzy thrusts. Thus Saucony's "Jazz," "Azura," and "Procyon"; Nike's "Air Skylon," "Air Humara" and "Air Terra Zori"; ASICS's "Kayano" and "Galileo"; Puma's "Inspire" and Converse's "Aspire." Often, shoes have the *same* name as cars, such as the Etonic "Nova," although Plymouth seems to be a favorite: e.g., the "Horizon" and the "Reliance." Another favored device is including the name of some patented technology the company has come up with: cell, gel, air, pod, pad, pump, flex, grind, grid, react, 2A, and so on. Sometimes a shoe plucks a tag from several different categories—for example, the Puma Cell Venom.

Some companies are deadly serious in naming. New Balance favors anodyne, serial number-ish strings, such as the "M1200WB," the "M866WG," or the particularly lilting "WCT645W," as if to say flashy names are sheer gimmickry and add unnecessary weight to the shoe. Other companies take a more playful approach, such as Reebok's two-part Allen Iverson launch, which provided "The Question" the first year and "The Answer" the second. ASICS puns its technology and global meteorology with the "GEL-Niño," while the names of the shoes in Converse's Chuck Taylor "Tribute Collection" read like the script for a growling boxing-match

NIKE EXECUTIVES WORRY about a potential backlash against the swoosh's omnipresence, or that over-saturation will weaken the brand. But for now the swoosh rushes ahead, speeding like capital across and above national borders, aligning itself with every sport in every country, as evidenced by a series of Nike T-shirts that show the swoosh and below a word such as "futbol," sold from London to Mexico City.

Street Knowledge

TECHNOLOGY ALONE does not drive shoe design. As a fashion icon, the sneaker is subject to fickle tastes and seasonally driven reinventions in the market. Design must incorporate the colors, styles, and influences bubbling amid youth culture which seem on the verge of spreading out to a wider audience—but not after they have already done so. "Now we're watching kids, whereas we used to watch designers," a Reebok product director told the *Wall Street Journal*. To chart the elusive style shifts, companies turn to a handful of trend-tracking and focus-group firms aimed at the teenage and children's market. Stationed in rave clubs and thrift stores, these firms—with names like Sputnik—poll youth consumer attitudes and alert companies to percolating movements. In *The New Yorker,* Malcolm Gladwell described the role these "cool-hunters" play as a sneaker company plans to issue new product:

from **"The Coolhunt,"** by Malcolm Gladwell, in *The New Yorker* (1997):

When [coolhunter] Baysie Wightman went to Dr. Jay's, she was looking for customer response to the new shoes Reebok had planned for the fourth quarter of 1997 and the first quarter of 1998. This kind of customer testing is critical at Reebok, because the last decade has not been kind to the company. In 1987, it had a third of the American athletic shoe market, well ahead of Nike. Last year, it had sixteen percent. "The kid in the store would say, 'I'd like this shoe if your logo wasn't on it,'" E. Scott Morris, who's a senior designer for Reebok, told me. "That's a kind of punch in the mouth. But we've all seen it. You go into a shoe store. The kid picks up the shoe and says, 'Ah, man, this is nice.' He turns the shoe around and around. He looks at the side and he goes, 'Ah, this is Reebok,' and says, 'I ain't buying this,' and puts the shoe down and walks out. And you go, 'You was just digging it a minute ago. What happened?'" Somewhere along the way, the company

promo: Desire. Courage. Skills. Instinct. Hype. Payback. Ancient history is represented by Adidas' "Forum," as well as Brooks' "Chariot" and "Gladiator." Newer companies such as Skechers, which cater to "alternative music" audiences and skateboarders, are off the map with shoes such as the "Gossip Pussycats," the "Euro-Pop Warp," and the "Pin-Up Betty."

Even more energy goes into naming the technology that will undergird the entire shoe line. In 1983, when the running boom was beginning to wind down, *Harper's* magazine took stock of the trademarked technologies the trend had spawned: "Nike has its 'Thermoplastic Heel Counter.' Etonic peddles the 'Dynamic Reaction Bar,' Tiger the 'Stabilizing Pillar,' Puma the 'dual-density Tri-Wedge system,' Saucony the 'Dutchman,' Brooks the 'Diagonal Rollbar,' and New Balance, prosaically, the 'Motion Control Device.'" Over a decade later, the companies had gone through several new lines of technology (another hint of Detroit:

last year's "rack-and-pinion steering" is this year's "realtime four-wheel drive"), and the new techniques were applied across the line, not just to running shoes. Saucony had its GRID ("Ground Reaction Inertia Device"); Reebok its DMX (condensation of "Dynamic Exchange"); Fila its carbon-Kevlar and mysterious "2A" system (a glyph for "to action" or "two action"); Puma its "Trinomic" and "Cell" technologies; ASICS Tiger its gel, "Wave Duo-Sole," and "Trusstic System," Brooks its silicone-based "Hydroflow ST." Components and materials such as Phylon, Abzorb, Stytherm, and AHAR round out the military-industrial mix.

This may all seem like window dressing, but it's worth paying attention to sneaker talk. When Nike filmed a commercial in Kenya featuring a Samburu tribesman speaking in his native Maa, a sharp-eared anthropologist in the United States discerned that he was really saying, "I don't want these. Give me big shoes." Now *there's* a slogan.

68

lost its cool, and Reebok now faces the task not only of rebuilding its image but of making the shoes so cool that the kids in the store can't put them down.

Every few months, then, the company's coolhunters go out into the field with prototypes of the upcoming shoes to find out what kids really like, and come back to recommend the necessary changes. The prototype of one recent Emmitt Smith shoe, for example, had a piece of molded rubber on the end of the tongue as a design element; it was supposed to give the shoe a certain "richness," but the kids said they thought it looked overbuilt. Then Reebok gave the shoes to the Boston College football team for wear-testing, and when they got the shoes back they found out that all the football players had cut out the rubber component with scissors. As messages go, this was hard to miss. The tongue piece wasn't cool, and on the final version of the shoe it was gone. The rule of thumb at Reebok is that if the kids in Chicago, New York, and Detroit all like a shoe, it's a guaranteed hit. More than likely, though, the coolhunt is going to turn up subtle differences from city to city, so that once the coolhunters come back the designers have to find out some way to synthesize what was heard, and pick out just those things that all the kids seemed to agree on. In New York, for example, kids in Harlem are more sophisticated and fashion-forward than kids in the Bronx, who like things a little more colorful and glitzy. Brooklyn, meanwhile, is conservative and preppy, more like Washington, D.C. For reasons no one really knows, Reeboks are coolest in Philadelphia. In Philly, in fact, the Reebok Classics are so huge they are known simply as National Anthems, as in "I'll have a pair of blue Anthems in nine and a half." Philadelphia is Reebok's innovator town. From there trends move along the East Coast, trickling all the way to Charlotte, North Carolina.

INSIDE THE FIRMS, designers distill larger fashion movements into the shoes themselves. Keds, the simplest sneaker but also a blank and inexpensive canvas on which to inscribe the latest value-added fashion, is particularly attuned to the runway: "Keds designers are on top of all the latest and future fashions," a spokeswoman told the *St. Louis Post Dispatch*. "So they do a lot of their own forecasting, while wanting to maintain core customers and get new, fashion-forward ones, too." As a result, designers ranging from Todd Oldham to Lilly Pulitzer have been imprinting flowers and leopard-skin on the shoes, to which platform soles are often affixed. The reason? A 23 percent sales drop in 1995 attributed largely to the improved fashion consciousness of other brands, ranging from Converse to Adidas to Candies. With the arrival of Oldham, the firm's president told *Footwear News,* "We are in the midst of revitalizing a great American brand. We want to enhance our fashion relevance by aligning with people with tremendous fashion credibility."

A similar desire drives shoe companies' forays into New York's 125th Street and other urban shopping strips, which are like living litmus tests to gauge a shoe's survival. The writer Josh Feit describes how Nike designers regularly sally out of the lab and into the streets to see how and where their product is landing:

from **"The Nike Psyche,"** by Josh Feit, in *Willamette Week* (1997):

For Aaron Cooper, whose long, rock-star hair, baggy shorts, Nike socks and 5 o'clock shadow give him the aura of a beach-bum philosopher, the definitive moment came when he first went what some marketers and designers call "bro-ing."

"Bro-ing" is industry chatter for going into the hood and saying, "Hey bro, want to check out some shoes?" It's a play on the term "pro-ing," or "pro-deal," which originated in the ski industry around the tradition of letting skiers test out new skis. Every three months, Nike introduces a dozen new basketball shoes, and it has become standard industry procedure for marketing and design staff to visit Philadelphia, Chicago, and New York with bags of samples to get reactions from ghetto kids.

Cooper, a white 26-year-old art-school grad from Pasadena who designs basketball shoes, claims that, for him, going into the city was more than market research. It opened his eyes about the importance of his product. "I don't want this to sound arrogant, because it's not that way," says Cooper, sitting in his workspace on the fourth floor of the Michael Jordan Building. In Harlem, Cooper says,

"We go to the playground, and we just dump the shoes out. It's unbelievable. The kids go nuts. That's when you realize the importance of Nike. Having kids tell you Nike is the number one thing in their life—number two is their girlfriend.

Some people see "bro-ing" as crass commercialism, especially because Nike shoes typically cost more than $100. Cooper sees it differently. "It's the broad scope of recognizing them as athletes, not just consumers."

YET ACCORDING TO THE NIKE ETHOS, there is no distinction between athlete and consumer, and so it is able to deflect criticism by presenting itself as a positive social force, not simply a marketer of expensive clothing.

If a sneaker company is not seeking the kids out in playgrounds, high schools, or skateboard parks, it can always round them up for focus-group sessions. For Vans, a shoe company once based around a few, simple, long-term models, rolling out new product with radically different uppers and soles is crucial for winning over consumers who are less interested in performance than in street credibility. The *Los Angeles Times* described a session where twelve local high-schoolers came to rate nearly two hundred prototypes for the Vans' fall line. Discussing Vans' design chief, the newspaper observed that she had for "the last six months conferred with three fashion and color forecasters, traversed much of Europe monitoring trends and kept apprised of the latest rages among the modish youth of Tokyo." The end result, the paper noted, was that "her sensibilities have spawned more varieties of Vans than were churned out during the 25 years before her arrival."

Reebok learned the hard way the penalty for taking its eye off the street. In January 1993, it released the "Shaq Attaq," the signature shoe of the Orlando Magic's then-rookie Shaquille O'Neal. White with blue trim and retailing for $130, the shoe withered on shelves in a season when black shoes were the rage and sneakers over a hundred dollars weren't selling. In 1997, Reebok, seeking to regain market share from Nike, pursued a different tack: focusing on the product. As *BusinessWeek* reported, CEO Robert Meers "stripped Reebok's marketers of control over design. Designers and manufacturing experts now work together on product-development teams—and Reebok marketers simply sell what they're given."

Of course, when talking about new sneaker launches, what is important is not simply what is coming out, but how it is coming out. In 1996, Converse, whose Chuck Taylor had made a comeback that lasted throughout the 1980s and early 1990s, sought a return to the basketball market. The company introduced two shoes—the All-Star 2000 and Dr. J, both of which had helped boost the company's sales 48 percent by the first quarter of the following year. Inspired by that success, the company planned a shoe endorsed by Dennis Rodman, the mercurial Chicago Bulls forward. Rather than just shipping it to stores, Converse put ten young part-time reps onto the streets in ten top urban markets, where they would distribute a small number of shoes and generally talk the brand up. As Jim Solomon, the head of marketing at Converse, told *USA Today*, there was more than just profit at stake.

"This brand needs life injected into it," he said. "We want edge and image. Market share will come with that." Three hundred thousand shoes were released, less than the company would hope to sell but certainly not a distribution oversight. "A limited roll-out makes kids hungry for the brand; it builds mystique," a Converse marketer told *USA Today*. "If everybody can get the shoe, it's no big deal." She added, "A shoe that's really smoking will sell out in about a week."

Converse's approach was hardly novel: earlier that year Reebok had trickled out five thousand pairs of "The Question," Allen Iverson's hundred-dollar name shoe, before releasing an initial shipment of 250,000. Similarly, Nike "allocates," in industry speak, limited numbers of Air Jordans to keep customers wanting. "That obviously is a way to control the supply and demand scenario," a Nike spokesman told the *New York Times*. The controlled rollouts and hype building have another, perhaps unintended effect: one New York sneaker store clerk was quoted as saying, "We stopped selling basketball shoes because the styles change so fast that a five-month-old pair of Nikes won't sell because they're not in style. Joggers are easier to deal with."

3

Executing the Play

Manufacturing and Distribution

"Our Chinese employees are exposed to Western business practices, ideas and beliefs, and dress, through their contact with Reebok."
—Reebok company official

"The issues... are wretchedly low wages, enforced over-time, harsh and sometimes brutal discipline and corporal punishment."
—Bob Herbert, *New York Times*

Whatever Happened to the Domestic Sneaker?

IN THE SPRING OF 1990, a storm-battered freighter, en route from Korea to the United States, spilled forty thousand pairs of Nike shoes into the Pacific Ocean. More than a year later, the shoes were washing up on the shores of Oregon. For oceanographers, the lost soles were a boon to the study of the ocean's currents. Yet the footwear flotilla was also a handy metaphor for the manufacturing and shipping patterns of athletic shoes, albeit at a much slower clip: following the flow of sneakers through the stormy seas of the "post-national" Asian economies, which produce more than 90 percent of the athletic shoes sold in the United States, is as complex a pursuit as the oceanographer's.

The production of modern "athletic shoes" has always had a minor presence in the United States. Domestic production has slipped from roughly 11 million to under 6 million in the last twenty years, while imports have surged dramatically. (See Figure 6) The rapid technological innovations and style shifts coming out of Europe and Japan in the late 1960s proved difficult for U.S. manufacturers to duplicate; when Converse, for example, tried in the late 1960s to produce its own leather basketball sneaker to compete with Adidas, the company faced problems in trying to produce the shoe in the typical vulcanized fashion. "The initial problems were that the leather tanners did not understand how to 'tan' leather for vulcanization," a Converse production head recalls in a company history. "They didn't understand our method and we didn't understand leather."

The imported shoes had another advantage: low-wage workers. As in the fashion industry, the manufacture of shoes has never been fully mechanized; materials tend to be fragile and the quick turnover of fashion doesn't lend itself well to investing heavily in fixed machinery that is only useful for one style. So the shoe industry relies on labor-intensive manual production. Cheap and plentiful labor, as well as low equipment and materials cost, has always been considered essential—making shoe production a perfect fit for developing nations. Just as the non-sneaker shoemaking industries shifted to Spain and Brazil in the 1960s and 1970s, athletic shoes once made in Germany or the United States were being made almost exclusively in Asia by the 1980s. Yet low wages alone do not explain why

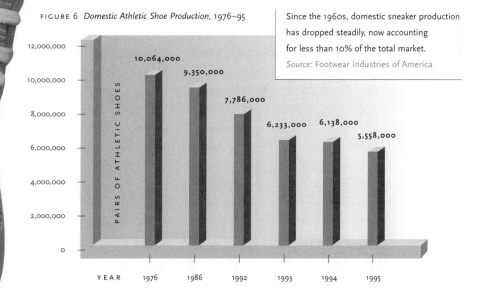

FIGURE 6 *Domestic Athletic Shoe Production, 1976–95*

Since the 1960s, domestic sneaker production has dropped steadily, now accounting for less than 10% of the total market.

Source: Footwear Industries of America

PAIRS OF ATHLETIC SHOES

12,000,000

10,000,000

8,000,000

6,000,000

4,000,000

2,000,000

0

10,064,000

9,350,000

7,786,000

6,233,000   6,138,000

5,558,000

YEAR   1976   1986   1992   1993   1994   1995

most shoe production has shifted to Southeast Asia; if wages were the only consideration, there is little reason they could not be produced in the United States. Indeed, one of the peculiar features of late twentieth-century economic life is that garment industry sweatshops are equally at home in the core as in the periphery. The journalist William Greider, writing about a toy factory fire in China, observed "one could not lament the deaths, harsh working conditions, child labor and sub-minimum wages in Thailand or across Asia and Central America without also recognizing that similar conditions have reappeared in the United States for roughly the same reasons." Asia offered other comparative advantages to sneaker production, perhaps most importantly a fully developed network of parts suppliers that simply did not exist in the United States.

Even though today's sneakers feature chemical company composites in the soles and an expanded range of material on the upper, their assembly has changed little over the past half-century. As one study points out, "although contingent upon specific styles and general types, the manufacture of athletic (and casual and dress) footwear consists of a few steps: i.e., designing, model and pattern making (which today involves chemical and tool engineering), material cutting, stitching, lasting, bottoming, and finishing, final inspection, and packaging... [T]o a large extent, shoe assembly centers—both literally and organizationally—around the last, a wooden, metal, or plastic form over which the semifinished upper is shaped."

By the mid-1970s, Converse, Puma, and others would be producing shoes in Yugoslavia, while Nike, which in its infancy was distributing the shoes of Japan's ASICS, was producing most of its shoes in Asia (it did, however, have factories in Exeter, New Hampshire, and Saco, Maine, until the early 1980s). The rubber industry, in the throes of the recession, along with shoe producers like Converse and Uniroyal, sought protection from cheap imports; Nike, meanwhile, was running anti-tariff ads that called on readers of *Runner's World* to "Help us get the U.S. government's big fingers out of the runner's pocket." It was a small-scale forerunner of the auto wars to come, when politicians would be smashing Japanese compact cars with sledgehammers. By the mid-1980s, the domestic rubber and sneaker industries were mostly gone.

A handful of companies still produce traditional sneakers—made from stitched canvas and vulcanized rubber—in the United States. Converse, for example, operates a plant in Lumberton, North Carolina (the state that had the lowest average hourly manufacturing wages in the 1980s, according to the Bureau of Labor Statistics), and built a new plant in 1994 in Mission, Texas, to help meet increased demand for its All-Star shoe. Yet with the characteristic tumultuousness of the contemporary sneaker industry, by August 1996, with sales of Chuck Taylor's lagging, the Lumberton plant laid off 165 workers and the staff, which numbered 1,200 two years earlier, was down to 700, according to the Raleigh *News and Observer*. While Converse officials see the "Made in the U.S.A." tag as essential to marketing the Chuck Taylor as an American icon, most of the shoe's canvas uppers are stitched at a *maquiladora* in Reynoso, Mexico, before being shipped back to the United States for assembly by the Lumberton plant's workers—primarily African American women. In southern California, Vans produces roughly one-quarter of its line—the more traditional vulcanized models—at a plant in Vista, which in the time-honored manner of American sneaker manufacturing is filled with machines heating rubber, presses rolling sheets of dyed canvas, and workers stitching uppers and gluing them to the rubber sole. In 1995, Vans closed a much larger factory in Orange County and began producing most of its shoes in South Korea; as Vans' CEO, Gary Schoenfield, told the *San Diego Business Journal*, a "cold cure" solvent (i.e., Benzene) used to produce the shoes in Asia is illegal here.

Although flexibility and speed are often cited as reasons for producing shoes in Asia, companies like Vans and Converse can put sneakers in stores within nine weeks, while shoes made in Asia generally take longer to reach the shelves. The main reason for the speed differential is that a new Chuck Taylor model involves a change in fabric, but not in sole; Asian shoes, meanwhile, may go through several structural overhauls in the course of a year. The quick turn-around is essential to a fashion-oriented shoe (sales of Chuck Taylors, for example, surged after models at a New York fashion show wore them as part of an overall "grunge" aesthetic). Yet even the more technologically sophisticated Asian-produced shoes, which presumably are intended less for fashion than for athletics (and thus have a longer shelf life), are being manufactured under ever tighter deadlines.

"In the old days, we would make one model and it'd run for 9 to 12 months," a Nike production head told the *Far Eastern Economic Review*. "Now we are changing models every week." Sneaker manufacturing points up an interesting anomaly that contradicts our usual perceptions of global trade: the simplest operations remain in the U.S. while the more complex manufacturing processes go abroad.

One company that has run counter to this trend is New Balance, which manufactures high-end running shoes in the Northeast and prominently features "Made in the U.S.A." in its advertising. In 1997, the company had about 820 manufacturing employees, and was growing according to a New Balance spokeswoman, Catherine Shepherd ("strange but true," *Sportstyle* observed, "*expanding* U.S. production"). There are several footnotes to the "Made in the U.S.A." reputation that New Balance enjoys, however. In the fall of 1997, anywhere from roughly a quarter to half of New Balance's shoes came from Asian subcontractors, due, says Shepherd, to 30 percent growth in sales over the previous four years. The amount of shoes coming from Asia "literally changes every week," Shepherd told me, "but we're trying to get back to where we were several years ago" in terms of U.S. production. In addition, even those shoes that are assembled here are often made using a variety of components shipped from abroad (for example, soles from China). This fact prompted the Federal Trade Commission, in 1994, to challenge the "Made in the U.S.A." claims of New Balance, as well as Hyde Athletic (maker of Saucony shoes); by 1996, however, the FTC reached tentative settlements with both companies, dropping its earlier complaint in return for the companies' agreement to not advertise all shoes as being U.S.-made. For its part, New Balance claims to be doing what it can to produce shoes here, but the rubber industries capable of producing the dense, technology-laden soles they need left in the 1970s and have no plans to return. "If companies like Nike and Reebok moved here," Shepherd argues, "the volume would be here."

Wages and subcontracting networks are not the only issues that determine what kind of sneakers are made here and what models are produced abroad. As the economic geographers James Austen and Richard Barff note, a complex and variegated tariff structure (known as the "Harmonized Tarriff Schedule") affects sneakers as any other product:

from **"It's Gotta Be Da Shoes,"** by James Austen and

Richard Barff in *Environment and Planning* (1993):

One of the most important issues in tariff variability is the manner in which the upper is attached to the sole of the shoe. There are three main types: non-molded, molded, and fox-banded (where a strip of material is attached around where the sole and upper meet in order to reinforce the bond). Non-molded shoes carry the lowest duty, fox-banded the highest. The materials of the upper are also critical to the assessment of the tariff, which increases from synthetic leather, through genuine leather, nylon and leather combined, to textiles. Variations in sole attachment combined with variations in upper material can produce large variation in tariff from the 6 percent applied to men's synthetic leather non-molded shoes, to the 8.5 percent on men's leather basketball shoes, to the 10.5 percent on nylon mesh running shoes to the 37.5-percent-plus 90-cents on canvas fox-banded shoes.

The differences in tariffs affect the geography of athletic footwear production. In the case of Converse, the geographic organization of production appears to be a direct result of the tariff system. Converse manufactures all of its fox-banded canvas shoe models in the United

States and subcontracts the production of its leather molded basketball shoes abroad. Furthermore, the cost of the shoe augments the duties on these two types of footwear: canvas athletic shoes are much cheaper to produce than leather ones, so a tariff represents a greater percentage of the total cost of a canvas shoe than of a leather shoe. Note also that the canvas uppers for Converse were stitched in a tariff-free maquiladora. Tariffs for imported textile uppers range from 9 percent-plus-thirty cents to 11.2 percent-plus-thirty cents. These tariffs are relatively large considering the importer's cost per stitched upper is about twenty-five cents.

Tariffs influence the geography of New Balance's production too. The company produces its running and court shoes (footwear with mesh, leather, and nylon uppers) in Maine and Massachusetts. Leather basketball and aerobic shoe production is subcontracted to firms in South Korea and Taiwan. Tariffs on basketball shoes average 8.5 percent; tariffs on running shoes start at 10.5 percent. Recall also that New Balance imports stitched uppers for several models of running shoe. They do this because the tariff on complete running shoes is over 10 percent: no tariffs are applied to imported nylon or leather uppers alone. New Balance therefore uses subcontractors to bypass the most expensive part of athletic footwear production (stitching) without having to pay tariffs.

To put it simply, Converse makes Chuck Taylor shoes in America because they are less labor intensive than specialized athletic shoes (which require much more stitching), and because the high tariff would make it too expensive to do it elsewhere. On the other hand, a 10 percent tariff on an expensive pair of running shoes represents a much smaller percentage of the total purchase price, and so it remains cost-effective for Nike and others to manufacture their shoes abroad. In the 1970s, Converse lobbied the U.S. government to keep tariffs high, while Nike did the opposite.

The Sneaker Capital of the World

BEHIND EVERY NIKE OR FILA SNEAKER is a complex web of design, manufacturing, and distribution stretching across dozens of countries. The Air Max Penny, for example, is a truly global product. As the *Far Eastern Economic Review* described it, the shoe is designed in Oregon and Tennessee (where Nike's "Air" technology is perfected), with input from technicians in South Korean and Taiwan. It is manufactured in South Korea and Indonesia with some fifty-two different components from five countries (the United States, Taiwan, South Korea, Indonesia, and Japan). During the assembly process, a single shoe is touched by some 120 pairs of hands.

With a handful of exceptions, the sneaker companies turn manufacturing over to subcontractors like the Taiwanese-run Yue Yuen factory in China's Pearl River Delta or Korean-owned PT Tong Yang in Indonesia; for this reason it has been suggested that firms such as Nike and Reebok are really "shoe marketers," not "shoe makers."

While the sneaker companies, particularly Nike, have been noted for their extremely horizontal integration and flexible networks of subcontractors, component suppliers, and "just-in-time" distribution and supply networks, they differ from some of the other so-called post-Fordist industrial operations at work in the global economy. Post-Fordist, or "flexible specialization" production involves vertically disintegrated networks of small-sized firms that share information; manufacturing takes place in small batches, using highly skilled workers who actively contribute to various stages of planning and assembly of the product. Nike, however, which uses low-skilled, low-wage labor in assembly-line production, is more properly thought of as a "neo-Fordist" company, Michael T. Donaghu and Richard Barff argue: "Nike's system of production has clearly moved beyond Fordist mass production with the complex subcontracting network and the production partnerships. Yet the company still relies on large volume production by semi- and unskilled labour." Nike is also somewhat unusual in that it opens or closes manufacturing operations without much regard to developing local markets: it closed U.S. factories as the market was increasing and opened facilities in countries where most of the shoes were exported. Canada's Bata, by contrast, has for years owned factories in several African countries, as well as in India, Indonesia, and other developing nations, where it relies on local labor to produce shoes largely for local markets.

Although Asian sneaker production originated in Japan, Taiwan, and South Korea, as wages and production costs have gradually risen most production has shifted to China, Indonesia, and Vietnam. For Nike, Indonesia and China now account for 70 percent of its production, while for Converse, more than 65 percent of its "performance" shoes are made in China. Not surprisingly, the Sporting Goods Manufacturing Association, which represents shoe and equipment companies, is one of the many special-interest groups that have lobbied yearly to renew China's Most Favored Nation status. As Converse senior vice president for sourcing Herb Rothstein told *Sportstyle*, a full revocation of MFN—and the hike in tariffs, from the current 3 to 10 percent to 35 to 45 percent—would have far-reaching effects in the industry: "The volume of business there in footwear and sporting goods is just too significant. There's no way to make up all the production elsewhere." Nike's spokesperson Donna Gibbs was more optimistic, however: the company would ship goods produced in China to Europe, she said, and utilize its Indonesian and Vietnamese facilities for the U.S. market.

The first major site of export-oriented athletic shoe manufacturing was South Korea, which throughout the late 1970s and 1980s dominated the manufacturing sphere. It featured low-wage, high-productivity workers; a strong government and weak labor unions; and an established network of raw materials and components suppliers. As late as 1990, Korea produced nearly 57 percent of the athletic shoes imported to the United States, according to *U.S. News & World Report*, but by 1994 it assembled only 14 percent. In his book *Just Do It*, Donald Katz describes Nike's arrival to South Korea and its eventual departure:

In 1974, Phil Knight made his famous South Korea visit, an event
that T. H. Lee and many others who watched the Korean
economy take off soon afterward regarded as something
like MacArthur's return to the Philippines or the arrival of
Commodore Perry in Tokyo Bay.

"I was there," T. H. said, climbing into one of the late-
model town cars that spirit Nike expatriates, or "expats," and
the travelers from the World Campus who arrive every few days
through the untenable traffic of Pusan. "I was the director of sales
at Sam Hwa when he came. We could only make typical canvas and
rubber sneakers at the time, Converse Chuck Taylors and the like.
But we knew that Mr. Knight and Blue Ribbon Sports were doing their
business in Japan, with Nippon Rubber and the others. We had a
relationship with Nippon Rubber, so we knew that the footwear
industry was beginning to transfer away from Japan—to us."

By the time Knight hired T. H. in 1982, Pusan factories were
turning out millions of athletic shoes by the month, and South Korea
had become the fastest growing economy in the world.

"It's hard to imagine how strange the comment seemed at the
time," said Whanil Jeong, the articulate president of the Dae Shine
Trading Company, one of the six high-tech shoe operations in Pusan
with which Nike was still doing business in June of 1993. "But in 1975,
when I went to work for Sam Hwa, the manager running my orientation
program warned us the Korean shoe business would not last long.
I was younger then. I thought the man was crazy."

"A plant like T3," T. H. Lee said as the black sedan pulled away from the factory that was churning out Carnivores, "it just didn't keep up. So soon we will stop doing business with T3 and there will be only five Nike factories in Korea."

T3 is owned by one of the many industrialists and leading politicians in South Korea known as President Park. Y. M. Park never went to college and worked his way up to his own factory from the stock-fitting line. His forty-eight-year-old brother, Y. C. Park, is the multimillionaire founder and president of T2—the Tae Gwang Industrial Company—a more technically advanced facility where most Air Jordans are still made. Another Park brother, Y. K., runs a factory that supplies Adidas and ASICS, and two other Park brothers also had their own shoe factories, both of which went bankrupt in 1991.

The Park brothers are extremely wealthy, though they live modestly by the standards of the internationally well-heeled, most of them still dwelling in apartments in Pusan. The Kims of Sam Hwa are extremely rich, as are the members of the Yang family that controlled the great Kukje plants. Several of the Taiwanese families that own Nike factories established after the Japanese passed along the production of athletic shoes are among the wealthiest families in Asia.

Political liberalization, burgeoning economic growth, and the rising cost of increasingly organized labor that often sends wages up 20 percent a year are usually pointed to as reasons that the Korean shoe industry is disappearing. "Some of these guys whose factories have closed put their profits in their pocket," however, as Nike's thirty-eight-year-old VP for production, a company rising star named Dave Taylor, has put it. "Some of them shut down their own doors during the 1980s and now only the most high-tech Korean shoemakers have survived."

After wages became prohibitive in South Korea and Taiwan, the sneaker companies initiated a push into Indonesia. Under President Suharto, Indonesia was seeking to boost export production to offset the falling oil revenues that had driven the country's rapid economic expansion over the previous two decades. In Indonesia, companies such as Nike and Reebok found conditions similar to South Korea or Taiwan in their heyday: an authoritarian government, low wages, weak labor unions, and the duty-free trade privileges of the General System of Preferences (GSP) allotted by the United States to developing nations (in 1989 South Korea and Taiwan were promoted to "newly industrialized countries").

For the most part, the shoe companies were dealing with the same South Korean subcontractors on Indonesian soil. As *Indonesia Business Weekly* reported in 1993, "Most Korean companies have moved their production lines to Indonesia. Most of their investments were channeled through joint ventures or in the form of technical assistance to Indonesian companies." The reason was clear, according to the newspaper. "Production costs here, according to industry sources, are approximately US$7 a pair. In South Korea, they are now approximately US$21.14 a pair." The rise of Indonesia's sneaker export economy was dramatic, from $23.4 million in U.S. dollars in 1987 to nearly a billion dollars in 1991, according to Indonesia's Central Bureau of Statistics. Indonesia's "comparative advantage" in the Pacific Rim was primarily cheap labor. Although Indonesia does have an indigenous rubber industry (like the sneaker industry, it is dominated by foreign firms— the Goodyear company opened a rubber plantation in Sumatra in 1916, hoping to get around the Brazilian rubber cartels), worth some $1.5 billion annually, it proved peripheral to the burgeoning shoe production, for several reasons: first, because most high-end athletic shoes produced today contain less than 10 percent rubber, according to PT Doson Indonesia; second, because the quality of local materials was often not up to industry standards. Unlike Korea, Indonesia lacked the component industries that support sneaker manufacture. "To make up-to-date shoes, you need to have satellite industries such as tanneries, textiles, plastic molding, iron-work moldings and others," said one manufacturer. As a result, roughly 75 percent of the materials used to produce the shoe, are imported from Korea, Taiwan, or Singapore. With low wages as the main attraction for doing business in Indonesia, the local producers had little leverage with U.S. companies. "That's why the sports shoe industry is usually described as a 'Buyer's Paradise.' They know exactly the production costs of each manufacturer. The producers do not have bargaining power at all," said another manufacturer. If the companies had little bargaining power, the workers had even less: Indonesia's one state-recognized union was described by the World Bank as "essentially a tightly-controlled government institution."

In the early 1990s, press accounts that documented violations of labor law and poor working conditions in the factories of foreign sneaker subcontractors began to drift back to the United States. If the Colombian coffee industry had Juan Valdez, the fictitious icon of the simple, happy coffee bean harvester, the Indonesian sports shoe industry had no convenient front. Instead it had Sadisah, a female Indonesian worker at the Sung Hwa Corporation, whose pay stub was documented by Press for Change's Jeffrey Ballinger in *Harper's*. Sadisah, according to Ballinger, was earning $1.03 a day, "which works out to just under 14 cents an hour, [which] is less than the Indonesian government's figure for 'minimum physical need' [a figure that was itself criticized, Ballinger noted elsewhere, because it used a 1956 'market basket' with woven sandals and straw mats for sleeping as its basis]." Cases of South Korean supervisors employing what Donald Katz called "management by terror"—that is, slapping female workers and putting them on forced runs—were also publicized. "Most Koreans are very hot-tempered, shouting, yelling, and hitting," J. Y. Park, a longtime Korean shoe worker in Indonesia was quoted as saying, but the real trouble is when they "try to treat Indonesians like Koreans." Meanwhile, papers such as *Media Indonesia* were running stories with headlines that read: "World Shoe Giants Rape Worker Rights." A U.S. Agency for International Development–funded study by the Asian-American Free Labor Institute found that more than 45 percent of the facilities were violating the minimum wage law, most often by implementing an illegal "training wage," which by 1994, Nike conceded, was still the going rate for a "large number of workers." As the World Bank and others have observed, enforcing minimum wages in the developing world is expensive, and little is often spent to do it. In Indonesia, the Legal Aid Institute told the *Indonesia*

Business Weekly that roughly 70 percent of companies had failed to pay the minimum wage in Jakarta and West Java. Back in the United States, the Made in the U.S.A. Foundation, made up of labor unions and domestic manufacturers, was advising consumers to "Send [Nike CEO] Phil [Knight] Your Shoes." Not only protectionists were antagonizing the sneaker companies; human rights groups and Christian organizations, among others, were seeking to improve conditions in Indonesia, not simply to bring jobs to the United States.

Under the increased scrutiny, including mention in a 1992 Human Rights report to the U.S. State Department, shoe companies were increasingly pressured to take action. The spotlight fell most harshly on Nike and Reebok, in part because of their market dominance and in part because their corporate image, built on anti-authority slogans and progressive social betterment through physical fitness, seemed so at odds with the accounts of underpaid employees stitching shoes seventy hours a week. They initially claimed the issue was in the hands of the subcontractors, but as the potential PR nightmare loomed larger they felt compelled to act. In 1992, Reebok instituted its "human rights production standards," while Nike issued a "Code of Conduct," which stated that "at every opportunity—whether in the design, manufacturing and marketing of products; in the environment; in the areas of human rights and equal opportunity; or in our relationships in the communities in which we do business—we seek to do not only what is required, but, whenever possible, what is expected of a leader." And so began a cycle: labor unions or rights groups would cite abuses, companies would take some action; more abuses would be cited, more actions would be taken, and so on. Yet as Press for Change's Ballinger notes, while companies continued to claim they could not know if abuses were going on, they nevertheless had the wherewithal to stop contractors from selling shoes "out the back door" into the gray market. There were other contradictions. Reebok, for example, gave a human rights award to a Chinese dissident and said high-mindedly that "profitability is not our only rationale for existence," but at the same time lobbied against the repeal of the Most Favored Nation status of China, a well documented abuser of human rights. As a company official told *The Nation*, making shoes *was* a way to improve the political and social situation: "Our Chinese employees are exposed to Western business practices, ideas and beliefs, and dress, through their contact with Reebok employees."

Marginal improvements have been made in the Jakarta-area minimum wage, due in part to hundreds of strikes over several years. While a Nike press release boasts that "history has proven that Nike's production can help build thriving economies in developing nations," the increase in the minimum wage was being bandied about as a sign for Nike to be moving on. Nike spokesperson Jim Small, quoted by Reuters, said of the wage hike that "there's concern [about] what that does to the market—whether or not Indonesia could be ... pricing itself out of the market."

There were places where the wages were even lower than in Indonesia, and the shoe companies' subcontractors were staking that territory out as well; not simply for wages, but for insurance against unforeseen developments in other locales. In China's Pearl River Delta, shoe production had risen steadily since the late 1980s, to the point where, by 1995, a Reebok manufacturing executive could tell *U.S. News & World Report* that China was poised to become the next South Korea of shoe production. The Pearl River Delta was filled with giants such as the Taiwanese-owned Yue Yuen Industrial Holdings, which employed some fifty-four thousand workers at three sites and produced 45 million pairs of sneakers in 1994. The largest factory at Dongguan, according to the *Far Eastern Economic Review*, "consists of eight separate low buildings, each containing dozens of production lines, up to 170 meters long. Each line bears the logo of the company for which its output is destined. The Nike lines are adorned with signs bearing the American firm's trademark exhortations like 'Just Do It!'" Unlike the firms in Indonesia, Yue Yuen sources out much of the sneaker materials itself. As one executive explained, "As cycles become shorter, we need to have control over all the materials. We need to be able to deliver in a shorter time and then we can get more orders."

In China, where independent unions are prohibited, similar allegations of labor law abuse were again surfacing. Anita Chan, researcher at the Australian National University, wrote in 1996 that at Yue Yuen, "conditions at this city-sized factory are above average for the district," but noted also that workers had illegal "enforced overtime" of eighty hours a month. In September 1997, the human rights watchdog Global Exchange released a survey of four manufacturers in the Pearl River Delta. The report, prepared by the Hong Kong Christian Industrial Committee and the Asia Monitor Resource Center, claimed that subcontractors were violating not just "the most basic tenets of Chinese labor law, they're also flagrantly violating [Nike's and Reebok's] own codes of conduct." At the Taiwanese-owned Nority plant in Dongguan, the report claimed, workers were making as little as $1.20 a day, below a required $1.90 minimum wage; while at a Korean-owned, Nike-producing Wellco plant, also in Dongguan, thirteen-year-old children were allegedly performing sewing and cutting work.

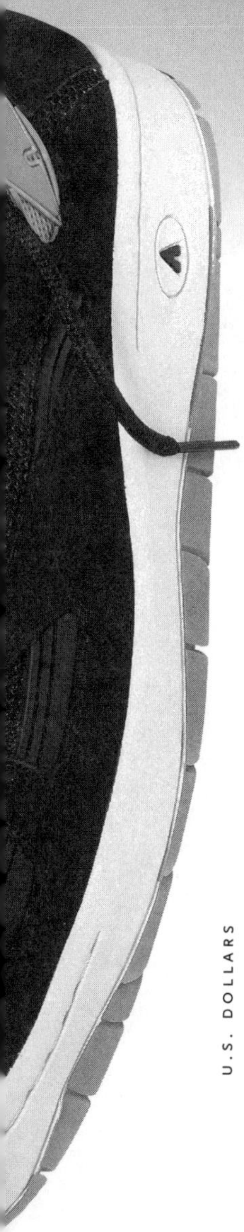

At Yue Yuen, the report said, workers were denied mandatory social security benefits and medical insurance. The companies,

FIGURE 7 *Hourly Wages for Footwear Production Workers,* 1992

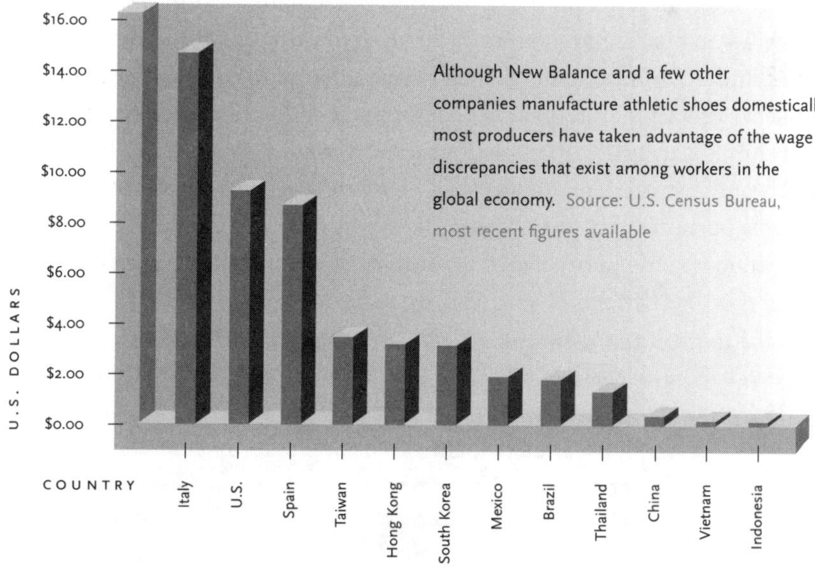

Although New Balance and a few other companies manufacture athletic shoes domestically, most producers have taken advantage of the wage discrepancies that exist among workers in the global economy. Source: U.S. Census Bureau, most recent figures available

meanwhile, continued to deny the charges; Reebok insisted they were not "Reebok factories," while Nike said the study "incorrectly states the wages earned by workers, [and] makes irresponsible accusations about worker health and safety."

A similar push was underway in Vietnam, where Nike was producing a million pairs of shoes a month using workers who often made the monthly minimum wage of forty-two dollars. Before the company discontinued the practice in May 1997, beginning workers—under the familiar "training wage"—had made only thirty-five dollars a month for the first ninety days, according to one report. As *U.S. News & World Report* observed, "with low wages and duty-free access to European markets, Vietnam could emerge as a major sneaker producer." For the sneaker companies, however, the rules of the game were a bit different in Vietnam. "[A]s Vietnam has thrown out the welcome mat to foreign investment," the *Journal of Commerce* reported, "Nike and other multinationals have encountered militant unions, strikes over wages and working conditions, and state-run newspapers that compete daily to cover the underside of market capitalism." When a Taiwanese supervisor at San Yang Vietnam Corp., the country's largest subcontractor, was charged in July with having forced fifty-six women to run the perimeter of the factory floor for wearing incorrect shoes (on International Women's Day, no less), he eventually received six months in prison; a leading Vietnamese newspaper, meanwhile, documented wage violations at the factory. Additional monitoring pressure came from émigré groups such as the New York–based Vietnam Labor Watch. Still, conditions were hardly ideal in Vietnam, according to an *Associated Press* dispatch from the state-owned An Lac Footwear Co., a factory outside Ho Chi Minh

City which had been a Bata factory before South Vietnam fell. "Even outside, the clatter of the factory's manual sewing machines is deafening. The summer sun shining down on the factory's corrugated metal roof can send the temperature inside soaring to nearly 100 degrees. Inside, ceiling fans whirl in a futile effort to cut the suffocating heat. Women are jammed along a series of assembly lines that churn out up to 7,000 pairs of shoes each day for Adidas, Fila, and All-Star."

The treatment of workers in Vietnam gained widespread attention in the United States after Garry Trudeau featured the issue in an eleven-part *Doonesbury* series, in 1997. Trudeau satirized, among other things, the wage differential between Nike endorser Michael Jordan and Nike's Vietnamese workers, as well as the legitimacy of fact-finding tours of Nike subcontractors' plants. In responding to Trudeau, Nike pointed to a recent fact-finding tour by former Atlanta mayor Andrew Young, who had, accompanied by Nike officials, toured the factories of Nike's Asian subcontractors. Young wrote, "It is my sincere belief that Nike is doing a good job in the application of its Code of Conduct. But Nike can and should do better." The *New York Times* columnist Bob Herbert, a fierce critic of Nike's labor policies, strongly questioned Young's findings. "The kindest thing that can be said at this point is that Mr. Young is naive," Herbert wrote. "He spent just three or four hours in each factory, and even he acknowledges that 'we probably should have insisted that we bring our own translators.'" Herbert said Young's claim not to have found child or prison labor was beside the point: "The issues ... are wretchedly low wages, enforced overtime, harsh and sometimes brutal discipline and corporal punishment."

Moreover, Young's report, the *New Republic* wrote, listed "consultants who were never consulted" and included "photos of union representatives who, it turns out, were not union officials."

Shortly after Young's report, Nike announced it would formulate a plan to act on and expand upon his recommendations. Reacting to continuing criticism over its labor practices, Nike released a company-funded report by researchers at Dartmouth University's business school who found that workers for Nike's Vietnamese subcontractors were paid a livable wage, and Nike announced a three-year program to provide low-interest loans to women who wanted to start their own businesses. While clearly intended as a response to the international criticism, it was unclear whether Nike and other companies would sincerely take up the issue of "living wages" directly (instead of leaving them to the vagaries of market behavior in the developing periphery), and whether "cultural differences" would continue to

Doonesbury

BY GARRY TRUDEAU

provide a handy way for sneaker companies to ultimately escape responsibility for those workers who unofficially made up the largest part of their workforce.

The Globetrotting Sneaker

The sneaker companies' tremendous profits over the past few decades have come thanks in part to continued access to low-cost labor in Southeast Asia. Not surprisingly, young women, roughly between the ages of eighteen and twenty-six, usually making roughly half the wages of their male counterparts, have formed the bulk of the sneaker assembly workforce. Cynthia Enloe, a Clark University professor, has documented how the movement of Asian women workers to organize for higher wages and more autonomy has intersected with the sneaker

Doonesbury   BY GARRY TRUDEAU

companies' push for higher profits, in the context of a global economy that equates having the choice to buy expensive athletic shoes (or other products) as a measurable improvement in the quality of life, even in countries where most citizens live in poverty. (In China, for example, Nike sells shoes at the U.S. equivalent of $59 to $78, according to the *Wall Street Journal*, while the average per-capita income was $190 in rural areas and $469 in urban areas in 1995.) Enloe writes:

from **"The Globetrotting Sneaker,"** by Cynthia Enloe, in *Ms.* (1995):

Four years after the fall of the Berlin Wall marked the end of the Cold War, Reebok, one of the fastest growing companies in United States history, decided that the time had come to make its mark in Russia. Thus it was with considerable fanfare that Reebok's executives opened their first store in downtown Moscow in July 1993. A week after the grand opening, store managers described sales as well above expectations.

Reebok's opening in Moscow was the perfect post–Cold War scenario: Commercial rivalry replacing military-posturing; consumerist taste homogenizing heretofore hostile peoples; capital and managerial expertise flowing freely across newly porous state borders. Russians suddenly had the "freedom" to spend money on U.S. cultural icons like athletic footwear, items priced above and beyond daily subsistence: at the end of 1993, the average Russian earned the equivalent of $40 a month. Shoes on display were in the $100 range. Almost 60 percent of single parents, most of whom were women, were living in poverty. Yet in Moscow and Kiev, shoe promoters had begun targeting children, persuading them to pressure their mothers to spend money on stylish, Western sneakers. And as far as strategy goes, athletic shoe giants have, you might say, a good track record. In the U.S. many inner-city boys who see basketball as a "ticket out of the ghetto" have become convinced that certain brand-name shoes will give them an edge.

But no matter where sneakers are bought or sold, the potency of their advertising imagery has made it easy to ignore this mundane fact: Shaquille O'Neal's Reeboks are stitched by someone; Michael Jordan's Nikes are stitched by someone; so are your room-mate's, so are your grandmother's. Those someones are women, mostly Asian women who are supposed to believe that their "opportunity" to make sneakers for U.S. companies is a sign of their countries' progress— just as a Russian women's chance to spend two month's salary on a pair of shoes for her child allegedly symbolizes the new Russia.

As the global economy expands, sneaker executives are looking to pay women workers less and less, even though the shoes that they produce are capturing an ever-growing share of the footwear market. And sneaker companies continue to refine their strategies for "global competi-tiveness"—hiring supposedly docile women to make their shoes, chang-ing designs as quickly as we fickle customers change our tastes, and shifting factories from country to country as trade barriers rise and fall.

The logic of it all is really quite simple; yet trade agreements such as the North American Free Trade Agreement (NAFTA) and the General Agreement on Tariffs and Trade (GATT) are, of course, talked about in a jargon that alienates us, as if they were technical matters fit only for economists and diplomats. The bottom line is that all companies

Sneakers and the Environment

Sneakers make nary a sound on the pavement, but do they tread so lightly on the environment? According to *Stuff: The Secret Lives of Everyday Things*, a report by the Northwest Environmental Watch (NEW) that documents what materials go into various everyday products, the manufacture of sneakers leaves a fairly heavy "footprint" on the ecosystem. For example, consider how much energy is used to ship raw materials to Asia, again to assemble the shoes, and again to ship finished product back to the United States. (NEW reports that shoes were the third-largest source of cargo for container ships going from East Asia to the U.S.)

Yet sneakers' biggest environmental impact comes from the industries that create the components that go into the shoes, NEW reports. Soles are made from ethylene vinyl acetate (EVA), a synthetic foam made from Saudi Arabian

operating overseas depend on trade agreements made between their own governments and the regimes ruling the countries in which they want to make or sell their products. Korean, Indonesian, and other women workers around the world know this better than anyone. They are tackling trade politics because they have learned from hard experience that the trade deals their governments sign do little to improve the lives of workers. Guarantees of fair, healthy, labor practices, of the rights to speak freely and to organize independently, will usually be left out of trade pacts—and women will suffer. The passage of both NAFTA and GATT ensured that a growing number of private companies will be competing across borders without restriction. The result? Big business will step up efforts to pit working women in industrialized countries against much lower-paid working women in "developing" countries, perpetuating the misleading notion that they are inevitable rivals in the global job market.

All the "New World Order" really means to corporate giants like athletic shoemakers is that they now have the green light to accelerate long-standing industry practices. In the early 1980s, the field marshals commanding Reebok and Nike, which are both U.S.-based, decided to manufacture most of their sneakers in South Korea and Taiwan, hiring local women. L.A. Gear, Adidas, Fila, and ASICS quickly followed their lead. In short time, the coastal city of Pusan, South Korea, became the "sneaker capital of the world." Between 1982 and 1989 the U.S. lost 58,500 footwear jobs to cities like Pusan, which attracted sneaker executives because its location facilitated international transport. More to the point, South Korea's military government had an interest in supplanting labor organizing, and it had a comfortable military alliance with the U.S. Korean women also seemed accepting of Confucian philosophy, which measured a woman's morality by her willingness to work hard for her family's well-being and to acquiesce to her father's and husband's dictates. With their sense of patriotic duty, Korean women seemed the ideal labor force for export-oriented factories.

U.S. and European sneaker company executives were also attracted by the ready supply of eager Korean male entrepreneurs with whom they could make profitable arrangements. This fact was central to Nike's strategy in particular. When they moved their production sites to Asia to lower labor costs, the executives of the Oregon-based company decided to reduce their corporate responsibilities further. Instead of owning factories outright, a more efficient strategy would be to subcontract the manufacturing to wholly foreign-owned—in this case, South Korean—

petroleum in Korean refineries. The leather upper is made from cowhides shipped from the United States to Asia, where the leather is tanned. The process once involved natural tannins, but now it's largely a chemical affair involving a solution made of agents such as calcium hydroxide. In Pusan, South Korea, NEW reports, "The tanning plant discharged hair, epidermis, leather scraps, and processing chemicals into the Naktong River." After the component parts of the sneakers make their way to an assembly plant in Indonesia, they are fastened together with a solvent-based toxic glue.

And then there's the box in which the sneakers are sold. The tissue in which they are wrapped, according to NEW, is made from trees that grew in the Sumatran rain forest. There has been some improvement on the box itself, at least for Nike: it's made of unbleached and recycled cardboard and is now held together with tabs and slots rather than petrochemical-based glue, as it had

103

been for years. The ink on the outside of the box, NEW reports, isn't made from heavy metals. Nike has made one other step to cut down on sneaker waste, NEW reports: its "Regrind" program, which takes excess rubber from one production cycle and blends it into the next, has cut down rubber consumption by 40 percent annually. There's yet no word on whether the pressurized-gas "Air" cushioning systems can be similarly recycled.

companies. Let them be responsible for workers' health and safety. Let them negotiate with newly emergent unions. Nike would retain control over those parts of sneaker production that would give its officials the greatest professional satisfaction and the ultimate word on the product: design and marketing. Although Nike was following in the footsteps of garment and textile manufacturers, it set the trend for the rest of the athletic footwear industry.

But at the same time, women workers were developing their own strategies. As the South Korean pro-democracy movement grew throughout the 1980s, increasing numbers of women rejected traditional notions of feminine duty. Women began organizing in response to the dangerous working conditions, daily humiliations, and low pay built into their work. Such resistance was profoundly threatening to the government, given the fact that South Korea's emergence as an industrialized "tiger" had depended on women accepting their "role" in growing industries like sneaker manufacture. If women re-imagined their lives as daughters, as wives, as workers, as citizens, it wouldn't just rattle their employers; it would shake the very foundations of the whole political system.

At the first sign of trouble, factory managers called in government riot police to break up employees' meetings. Troops sexually assaulted women workers, stripping, fondling, and raping them "as a control mechanism for suppressing women's engagement in the labor movement," reported Jeon-Lim Nam of Hyosung Women's University in Taegu. It didn't work. It didn't work because the feminist activists in groups like the Korean Women Workers Association (KWWA) helped women understand and deal with the assaults. The KWWA held consciousness-raising sessions in which notions of feminine duty zand respectability were tackled along with wages and benefits. They organized independently of the male-led labor unions to ensure that their issues would be taken seriously, in labor negotiations and in the pro-democracy movement as a whole.

The result was that women were at meetings with management, making sure that in addition to issues like long hours and low pay, sexual assault at the hands of managers and health care were on the table. Their activism paid off: in addition to winning the right to organize women's unions, their earnings grew. In 1980, South Korean women in manufacturing jobs earned 45 percent of the wages of their male counterparts; by 1990, they were earning more than 50 percent. Modest though it was, the pay increase was concrete progress, given that the gap between women's and men's manufacturing wages in Japan, Singapore, and Sri Lanka actually *widened* during the 1980s. Last but certainly not least, women's organizing was credited with playing a major role in toppling the country's military regime and forcing open elections in 1987.

Without that special kind of workplace control that only an authoritarian government could offer, sneaker executives knew that it was time to move. In Nike's case, its famous advertising slogan—"Just Do It"—proved truer to its corporate philosophy than its women's "empowerment" ad campaign, designed to rally women's athletic (and consumer) spirit. In response to South Korean women workers' newfound activist self-confidence, the sneaker company and its subcontractors began shutting down a number of their South Korean factories in the late 1980s and early 1990s. After bargaining with government officials in nearby China and Indonesia, many Nike subcontractors set up shop in those countries, while some went to Thailand. China's government remains nominally Communist. But both are governed by authoritarian regimes who share the belief that if women can be kept hard at work, low paid, and unorganized, they can serve as a magnet for foreign investors.

The 1994 Beijing conference also provided an important opportunity to call world attention to the hypocrisy of the governments and corporations doing business in China. Numerous athletic shoe companies followed Nike in setting up manufacturing sites throughout the country. This includes Reebok—a company claiming its share of responsibility for ridding the world of "injustice, poverty, and other social ills that gnaw away at the social fabric," according to a statement of corporate principles.

Since 1988, Reebok has been giving out annual human rights awards to dissidents from around the world. But it wasn't until 1992 that the company adopted its own "human rights production standards"—after labor advocates made it known that the quality of life in factories run by its subcontractors was just as dismal as that at most other athletic shoe suppliers in Asia. Reebok's code of conduct, for example, includes a pledge to "seek" those subcontractors who respect workers' rights to organize. The only problem is that independent trade unions are banned in China. Reebok has chosen to ignore that fact, even though Chinese dissidents have been the recipients of the company's own human rights award. As for working conditions, Reebok now says it sends its own inspectors to production sites a couple of times a year. But they have easily "missed" what subcontractors are trying to hide— like 400 young women workers locked at night into an overcrowded dormitory near a Reebok-contracted factory in the town of Zhuhai, as reported in the *Asian Wall Street Journal Weekly*.

Nike's co-founder and CEO Philip Knight has said that he would like the world to think of Nike as "a company with a soul that recognizes the value of human beings." Nike, like Reebok, says it sends in inspectors from time to time to check up on work conditions at its factories; in Indonesia, those factories are run largely by South Korean subcontractors. But according to Donald Katz in a book on the company, Nike spokesman Dave Taylor told an in-house newsletter that the factories are "[the subcontractors'] business to run." For the most part, the company relies on regular reports from subcontractors regarding its "Memorandum of Understanding," which managers must sign, promising to impose "local government standards" for wages, working conditions, treatment of workers, and benefits.

In April 1995, the minimum wage in the Indonesian capital of Jakarta was $1.89 *a day*—among the highest in a country where the minimum wage varies by region. And managers are required to pay only 75 percent of the wage directly; the remainder can be withheld for "benefits." By now, Nike has a well-honed response to growing criticism of its low-cost labor strategy. Such wages should not be seen as exploitative, says Nike, but rather as the first rung on the ladder of economic opportunity that Nike has extended to workers with few options. Otherwise, they'd be out "harvesting coconut meat in the tropical sun," wrote Nike spokesman Dusty Kidd, in a letter to the *Utne Reader*. The all-is-relative response craftily shifts attention away from reality: Nike didn't move to Indonesia to help Indonesians; it moved to ensure that its profit margin continues to grow. And that is pretty much guaranteed in a country where "local standards" for wages rarely take a worker over the poverty line. A 1991 survey by the International Labor Organization (ILO) found that 88 percent of women working at the Jakarta minimum wage at the time—slightly less than a dollar a day—were malnourished.

A woman named Riyanti might have been among the workers surveyed by the ILO. Interviewed by the *Boston Globe* in 1991, she told the reporter who had asked about her long hours and low pay: "I'm happy working here.... I can make money and I can make friends." But in fact, the reporter discovered that Riyanti had already joined her coworkers in two strikes, the first to force one of Nike's subcontractors to accept a new women's union and the second to compel managers to pay at least the minimum wage. That Riyanti appeared less than forthcoming about her activities isn't surprising. Many Indonesian factories have military men posted in their front offices who find no fault with managers who tape women's mouths shut to keep them from talking among themselves. They and their superiors have a political reach that extends far beyond the barracks. Indonesia has all the makings for a political explosion, especially since the gap between rich and poor is widening into a chasm. It is in this setting that the government has tried to crack down on any independent labor organizing—a policy that Nike has helped to implement. Referring to a strike in a Nike-contracted factory, Tony Nava, Nike representative in Indonesia, told the *Chicago Tribune* in November 1994 that the "troublemakers" had been fired. When asked about Nike policy on the issue, spokesman Keith Peters struck a conciliatory note: "If the government were to allow and encourage independent labor organizing, we would be happy to support it."

Indonesian workers' efforts to create unions independent of government control were a surprise to shoe companies. Although their moves from South Korea have been immensely profitable, they do not have the sort of immunity to activism that they had expected. In May 1993, the murder of a female labor activist outside Surabaya set off a storm of local and international protest. Even the U.S. State Department was forced to take note in its 1993 worldwide human rights report, describing a system similar to that which generated South Korea's boom 20 years earlier: severely restricted union organizing, security forces used to break up strikes, low wages for men, lower wages for women—complete with government rhetoric celebrating women's contribution to national development.

Yet when President Clinton visited Indonesia in November 1994, he made only a token effort to address the country's human rights problem. Instead, he touted the benefits of free trade, sounding indeed more enlightened, more in tune with the spirit of the post–Cold War era than do those defenders of projectionist trading policies who coat their rhetoric with "America first" chauvinism. But "free trade" is hardly *free* for any workers—in the U.S. or abroad— who have to accept the Indonesian, Chinese, or Korean workplace model as the price of keeping their jobs.

The not-so-new plot of the international trade story has been "divide and rule." If women workers and their government in one country can see that a sneaker company will pick up and leave if labor demands prove more costly than those in a neighbor country, then women workers will tend to see their neighbors not as regional sisters, but as competitors who can steal their precarious livelihoods. Playing women off against each other is, of course, old hat. Yet it is as essential to international trade politics as is the fine print in GATT.

But women workers allied through networks like the Hong Kong–based Committee for Asian Women are developing their own post–Cold War foreign policy, addressing women's needs: how to convince fathers and husbands that a woman going out to organize meetings at night is not sexually promiscuous; how to develop workplace agendas that respond to family needs; how to work with male unionists who push women's demands to the bottom of their lists; how to build a global movement.

These women refuse to stand in awe of the corporate power of the Nike or Reebok or Adidas executive. Growing numbers of Asian women today have concluded that trade politics have to be understood by women on their own terms. They are ready to engage with women from other regions to link the politics of consumerism with the politics of manufacturing. If women in Russia and Eastern Europe can challenge Americanized consumerism, if Asian activists can solidify their alliances, and if U.S. women can join with them by taking on trade politics—the post–Cold War sneaker may become less comfortable.

IN LATE 1997, the workers who assemble the shoes of Nike and other U.S. and European companies had more to worry about than simply low wages. The fiscal crises sweeping through Asia had knocked currencies such as the Indonesian rupiah down by more than half. U.S. companies had hoped Asian consumers would help ameliorate the effects of a slowdown in the domestic market, but now they could only watch as orders plummeted and retail stock accumulated.

FIGURE 8 *Why a Pair of Nike Pegasus Costs $70*

Athletic shoe companies are hesitant to disclose cost breakdowns in the manufacture of their products, but the *Washington Post* assembled information in 1995 about a pair of Nike Air Pegasus, priced at seventy dollars retail. Note that the cost of labor represents just one-third the cost of materials and just over half the amount spent on advertising and promoting the shoe. Source: *Washington Post, 1995*

Production Labor	$2.75	Research and Development	$0.25	Retailer's Rent	$9.00
Materials	$9.00	Promotion and Advertising	$4.00	Personnel	$9.50
Rent, Equipment	$3.00	Sales, Distribution, Admin.	$5.00	Other	$7.00
Supplier's Operating Profit	$1.75	Nike's Operating Profit	$6.25	Retailer's Operating Profit	$9.00
Duties	$3.00				
Shipping	$0.50				
Cost to Nike	**$20.00**	**Cost to Retailer**	**$35.50**	**Cost to Consumer**	**$70.00**

In Indonesia, over 6,000 workers went on strike at one factory upon learning job losses were imminent due to a reduction by Nike in its monthly orders.

Suddenly, the much-touted cycle of rising wages for workers and the eventual creation of a consuming middle-class seemed to be out of order. In 1989, Thailand was Nike's second-largest manufacturing base, according to *Fortune*. By 1997, wages had risen nearly 80 percent and the company had long moved its operations elsewhere. Now Thailand was expected to be a market for Nike shoes, a plan that had been proceeding apace until the 1997 economic meltdown. Suddenly Mercedes-Benz dealers were cutting prices in half and purchases of sneakers, like everything else in Thailand, had dropped. In response, Nike planned a series of ads that would be sensitive to the financial crisis yet still embolden Thai consumers—at least enough to purchase sneakers. The sneaker companies' woes in Asia were compounded by continuing criticism of the labor conditions in their Asian subcontractors' factories, with industry leader Nike continuing to bear the brunt of the criticism. Film maker Michael Moore, in *The Big One*, challenged Nike CEO's Phil Knight's assertion that Americans would take a sneaker manufacturing job by arranging rallies in Flint, Michigan and other economically depressed locales where unemployed or underemployed residents stated they would indeed be glad to make sneakers (after all, New Balance and Hyde, makers of Saucony, seemed to have had no trouble finding workers). After an Ernst and Young survey of Nike's factories in Vietnam that indicated labor law violations was leaked to the press, the issue was broached in Congress.

The criticism spread beyond the usual labor and human rights watchdogs. Students at the University of North Carolina protested the school's $7.1 million affiliation with Nike on the grounds of the company's labor policies; the company promised to take four students on a factory tour in return. Green Bay Packer All-Pro lineman Reggie White, paid by Nike to wear the company's shoes, said Nike would "rather hire the cheap labor than hire the kid in the neighborhood who is buying the shoes." Former N.F.L. player David Meggyesy blasted Tiger Woods, Jerry Rice, and Michael Jordan, calling them "moral jellyfish" for their refusal to take any accountability for their employers' actions and policies: "Not protesting Knight's $5 billion and Jordan's $20 million stacked against a Vietnamese worker's $1.60 per day is flat out immoral. Shilling for $140 sneakers that cost $3.50 to make is equally immoral. If Jordan, Rice, Agassi and Woods feel no shame at taking Nike's blood money, what will shame them?" Meggyesy lamented the superstars' lack of "social accountability," their willingness to pass the buck to Nike or Reebok. They were acting in much the same fashion as their sneaker company employers, who because they did not directly hire their own assembly workers (preferring to let the subcontractors do the labor law violating and low-wage paying) were kept comfortably insulated from demands by those workers or violations of labor laws.

4

The Cheerleaders

Advertising and Marketing

"Nike is a marketing-oriented company, and the product
is our most important marketing tool."
—Phil Knight, CEO of Nike

How to Sell a Sneaker

IN 1995, SNEAKER COMPANIES spent an average of 9.7 percent
of sales on marketing, or nearly $800 million, according to the
Sporting Goods Marketing Association. In 1990, the figure had been
6.8 percent. While this proportion is roughly similar to that found
in the advertising of other consumer products and industries, it is
noticeably higher than the average amount—3.8 percent—spent to
advertise nonathletic footwear.

Simply put, sneakers have become more like fashion items or
personal technology products than shoes. Where a consumer is
probably more motivated to buy a pair of nonathletic shoes by need—
whether for work, school, or a formal occasion—the need for
sneakers is not as clearly defined. For children, they are the
default shoe, which in itself does not explain why so many
children own so many pairs of sneakers at the same time, or
why they need shoes with high-performance features.
(According to Simmons Market Research Bureau, kids 6 to 14
bought on average three pairs of sneakers in a year; sneaker
spending was the highest of any clothing category.) For adults,
beyond the professional or at least serious amateur athlete,
the need is even less apparent, at least in a material sense.
So the shoe companies shift the selling point away from the
product itself and into a world of their own making: a world of
inspirational, predawn runs; a grainy black-and-white universe
of women in boxing gyms who are not simply sparring but reaching

into new metaphysical territory; a colorful, crazy-camera-angle realm where life is a big skateboard park lived to the "extreme"; a sepia-toned storehouse in which one can rediscover what is simple and good about life.

Achieve. Commitment. Life is Not a Spectator Sport. There Is No Finish Line. Just Do It. Change the Game. Knowing that the majority of people do not "just do it" when it comes to physical fitness, the shoe ads reward those who do it and hold out hope to those who don't that there is a path toward self-improvement, an athletic absolution made possible through the strength of one's character and the performance features of a new cross-training shoe. The relationship is pitched as one to one: shoe company confiding to you that *here is a way.* That you *can* do it. This is why shoe ads, even the ones that feature famous athletes, almost always depict their subjects engaged in solitary, man-against-forces-of-gravity quests in some dingy gym or desolate peak, back where it all began, back where it all matters, away from the hype and the pretenders to the throne. Whether Michael Jordan really broods in dark gyms shooting free throws is not the issue; the issue is the individual taking on his own short-comings, conquering weakness and becoming a better person. Not with the help of a teammate (who might wear a different brand of shoe), but bolstered by one's own inner strength. The messages are vague yet positive; we're not really sure what we are supposed to "achieve" or what game we're supposed to change or even what we're supposed to do when we "just do it," but it's a message that speaks to more people than would "Run Faster in the 100M" or "Jump Higher in the Steeplechase."

Evidence is murky at best that advertising alone impels a consumer to purchase a given product, but if there were a case to be made for its importance it would be in the sneaker industry. Interestingly, none of the major companies used much advertising at all during their initial ascendance, but to reach beyond the narrow athletic market they eventually turned to Madison Avenue. Stitches and glue may hold the shoe together, but it is advertising that assembles an identity, imparts a psychic meaning, and endows transformative power to an ultralight batch of plastic and nylon. Sneakers are walking agglomerations of intellectual property: the multiplying swooshes, formstripes, and vectors on the side, tongue, and back; the trademarked Phylons and Grid systems, whose formulas are zealously guarded; the names that excite the imagination and are

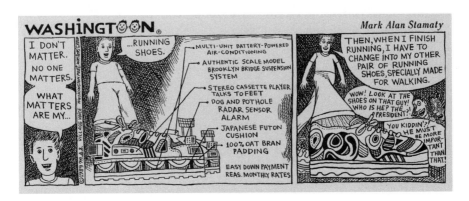

WASHINGTOON®   Mark Alan Stamaty

I DON'T MATTER. NO ONE MATTERS. WHAT MATTERS ARE MY...

...RUNNING SHOES.

- MULTI-UNIT BATTERY-POWERED AIR-CONDITIONING
- AUTHENTIC SCALE MODEL BROOKLYN BRIDGE SUSPENSION SYSTEM
- STEREO CASSETTE PLAYER TALKS TO FEET
- DOG AND POTHOLE RADAR SENSOR ALARM
- JAPANESE FUTON CUSHION
- 100% OAT BRAN PADDING

EASY DOWN PAYMENT REAS. MONTHLY RATES

THEN, WHEN I FINISH RUNNING, I HAVE TO CHANGE INTO MY OTHER PAIR OF RUNNING SHOES, SPECIALLY MADE FOR WALKING.

WOW! LOOK AT THE SHOES ON THAT GUY! WHO IS HE? THE PRESIDENT?

YOU KIDDIN'?! HE MUST BE MORE IMPORTANT THAN THAT!

whispered reverently, just as in car ads. That the shoes of different companies roll off production lines in the same building in China's Pearl River Delta is evidence enough that there isn't anything substantially different about the shoes themselves, but that $800 million a year is intended to manufacture the illusion of difference.

With the brash, iconoclastic rebel-turned-near-monopolistic-market-giant Nike dominating the industry (at least for now), outspending their competition on marketing by at least two to one, "positioning"—that is, creating an identity discernible from Nike's—becomes crucial. So Converse hires focus groups who tell the company they value its history, and an ad featuring basketball "Hall of Famers" follows. Adidas, meanwhile, makes a play for the hardcore jock. "A lot of people here know us as the soccer brand or the retro-fashion brand or the rapper brand," an Adidas marketer told *Shoot*. "But what we are really is a multisport company that caters to athletes, and that's the message we have to get out there with." Fila, meanwhile, goes

with the Detroit Pistons' forward Grant Hill dancing in a tuxedo. "What we're saying is that you don't have to give up fashion to get function, and vice versa," a Fila executive told *Shoot*.

Sneakers and Nothingness

The question becomes: How can a company maintain its brand's "core equities"—those images, qualities, and associations at the heart of its identity—while still expanding to meet new product lines and new markets? The last decade or so is filled with missteps: Nike's disastrous entry into the "casual shoe" market, or Keds' ill-fated attempt to enter the performance market. Sometimes, a rise in sales has nothing to do with any concerted effort, as when the first "Old School" rappers began wearing Puma Clydes or old Adidas shoes; or when Sean Penn's character slapped a pair of checkered Vans against his head in *Fast Times at Ridgemont High*, launching an unplanned flurry of sales activity. But shoe companies don't want accidents, they want sales, and so 10 percent of those sales go to crafting a Jordan or Agassi-sized image and empowering aura around what may just be a comfortable shoe in which to play tennis. In the excerpt below, the advertising critic Leslie Savan shows how a slew of shoe campaigns work to make a sneaker purchase an act of the soul, not just the sole:

from **The Sponsored Life**, by Leslie Savan (1994):

Nike, Reebok, BKs, Cons, Keds, ASICS, Etonic, even L.A.-softened
Gear—like the basic sex words, sneaker names punch their
presence into the world with a lot of guttural, aggressive
K sounds. (And look how "sneakers" kicked the soft ass
of "tennis shoes," which so many of us non–East Cost types
grew up calling them.) Sneaker identities hoist themselves
into being out of nothingness, meaning embossed like logos
on leather. The same goes for sneaker ads, which try to
convince us that there's an innate relationship between a brand
and an attitude. It's a relationship that goes poof in the night
with each new ad agency a company hires (are Reebok buyers Bungee
murderers, whimsical U.B.U. surrealists, or powerful Pumpin' real guys?).
And yet out of this nothingness, out of a market that barely existed two
decades ago, arises a huge industry; and urgency that, yes, some kids
killed for; and second homes for college coaches who convince their players
to model product.

As today's aspiring white Negroes—Mailer's late '50s label for white
hipsters who "absorbed the existential synapses of the Negro"—strive
to imitate black male athletes (Nike says 87 percent of its domestic athletic
shoes are sold to whites), sneakers tease all men with the possibility of
making hipness out of nothingness. Sometimes women get play too,
as Nike helps us to become an eight-page spread that ends with "Because
you know it's never too late to have a life. And never too late to change one.
Just do it." That the most existential tag line in history comes from a
sneaker company is pretty fuckin' K itself.

For both companies and consumers, sneakers are about defining yourself, becoming yourself through slogan, logo, and look. For now, number-one Nike defines what defining yourself is. How does a manly shoe compete?

Out-cooling Nike is an obvious answer and some have tried, but lately the strategy has been to become more aggressively K. Attacks on Nike—by Reebok, BK, ASICS, and L.A. Gear—have created a confusing shoe-off. First ASICS, a Japanese company that is number three in the world but only 10th in the U.S., came out with an ad that said, compared to its GEL-Spotlytes, "Everything else is just hot air." (A superimposed slogan rubbed it in: "Do It Better.") The networks asked ASICS to tone it down to "Anything more is a lot of hot air." Still ABC refused to run the spot—even while running L.A. Gear's ad in which hoops star Karl Malone slow-growls, "Everything else is just hot air."

"Money talks," explains a spokeswoman at ASICS, which spends $5 million a year in advertising while L.A. Gear spends $70 million. ASICS asked for compensation from ABC and considered action against L.A. Gear. But that's not all. Gear's agency, BBDO, quit in disgust over Gear's meddling into ad making, including its insistence on "hot air," which the agency thought was cheesy. Pivoting, BBDO eyed Reebok, which was frustrated with its agency HHCC. Reebok had already farmed out its Pump ads to another suitor, George "I want my MTV" Lois. (Finally, Reebok gave the remainder of its business to its former agency Chiat/Day/Mojo.) Pump tries to slam-dunk Nike with the tag line "Pump Up and Air Out."

It may seem odd, but besides manhood, sneaker companies are also hauling mothers into their ads: David Robinson's for Nike, Isiah

Thomas's for ASICS, and "your mother" for British Knights. Moms anchor a guy, illustrate his heart, and yet serve to provide higher contrast between his toughness and the softer female world. The Nike and ASICS spots are lovable portraits, but BK took up the playground challenge and just blurted it out: "your mother wears Nike."

The new slogan doesn't make Nike equal to army boots (that would be only too fine nowadays); instead it equates Nike with a bunch of middle-aged suburban ladies talking about plastic surgery and "top restaurants" while they play tennis in their Nikes. The poor ladies are crucified in order to define what BK isn't. The tack is similar to the savvy savagery that the same agency,

FIGURE 9 *Global Marketing Spending for Three Leading Companies, 1994-1997*

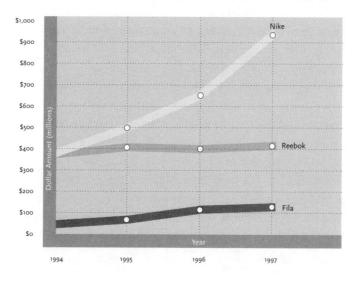

The "tyranny of the swoosh" hasn't come cheaply, as Nike now outspends its nearest competitor two to one. Source: Salomon Brothers, Sporting Goods Intelligence

Deutsch, lobbed at the Japanese in its Pontiac dealer ads ("If you're still thinking about buying a Japanese car," threatens a grizzly voiceover, "...maybe you should move to Tokyo") and at the real, mainly Jewish and working-class furniture movers in IKEA furniture spots ("Do you even need these guys?" the narrator asks dismissively).

Deutsch is a pro at toppling buying resistance with a dash of stereotype, but sees its BK campaign as "authentic rebellion." "Nike is authentic sports," an agency man there told me. "They've pre-empted it. It's tough for any competitor to break through that. So we went for authentic rebellion."

Authentic is where the arc is pointed. Converse recently announced "the largest and most comprehensive ad campaign in its 84-year history," featuring the slogan, "It's what's inside that counts." After eight months of research, Converse came up with "six key adjectives" to describe its "brand personality": "confident, genuine, hardworking, tough, unselfish, and passionate." And so the measure of one's authenticity is not brash bravado but a kind of rawness gnawing through Converse's new print ad: "You can always spot a guy who wears Cons. Not by what's on his feet"—that would be too easy—but rather, by what's in his soul. *He eats pain.*"

Like Converse endorser Bernard King, who came back from major knee surgery to his best season ever, and who said, at least for a Converse press release, "It's the voice inside that makes the difference in your life. Whether it's the kind of things you hear from your parents when you're growing up or what the doctors tell you after knee surgery. You're the one who has to decide to make it work and work well."

The language is true and good, and even turns on an existential moment—until he finishes in the dialect of the sponsored life: "The new Converse campaign says it perfectly for all aspects of life: It's what's inside that counts."

///////////////////////////////

In 1968, the Converse company—whose product was worn by nearly 90 percent of the nation's professional basketball players—spent about three hundred thousand dollars on advertising, according to its company history. By 1978, that figure had increased ten times, to $3 million. By the next decade, ad budgets for sneaker companies would be in the tens of millions.

The spending accelerated in the mid-1980s after former market leader Nike found itself trailing upstart Reebok and its fashionable aerobic shoes. Air Jordan was the first step: Nike spent $5 million between 1984 and 1986 advertising the new colored leather shoe, in the process helping Jordan to transcend his Chicago market and emerge as a national icon. But Air Jordan was only one vessel in the advertising armada launched against Reebok. In March 1987, Nike released a ten-model "Air" line meant to stress the company's commitment to athletes and serious performance over fashion. Bolstered by an estimated $20 million advertising budget, Nike began its assault, most infamously with a television campaign that featured a Super-8 montage of shoe and athletes set to the Beatles' song "Revolution"—a move that drew a copyright-infringement lawsuit from Apple Records. It wasn't the first time the company brashly announced its anti-establishment status and co-opted images of rebellion, and it wouldn't be the last: Nike would later issue a commercial set to the Stooges' "Search and Destroy," a song originally intended as a Vietnam War protest. Revolution now was a slippery buzzword for breaking your own personal limits in sports, tweaking the established order of a given sport (or society), or buying a product that set you apart from the herd of majority opinion, which was a tall order inasmuch as that company *was* the majority.

The "Air" attack marked a sea change in the character of the company, as well as the amount of its ad spending. "We expect a good year," a Nike spokesman told *Advertising Age* in 1988, "and I guess we're admitting that maybe traditional [mass market] advertising works." The sales figures backed it up: orders went up some 30 percent, while profits more than doubled during the first half of the fiscal year. The company told retailers its overall $34 million ad budget for 1988 was four times the television spending and three times the print spending over the previous year. Reebok quickly countered Nike's advance, spending nearly $20 million in the last half of 1988 alone. Yet where Reebok's ad campaign—centered around the theme that Reebok shoes let "U.B.U."—fizzled (Keds later spoofed it with the picture of a sixty-five-dollar pair of Reeboks and the tag line "U Gotta B Kidding") and is largely a footnote today, Nike's ad campaigns landed in the cultural vernacular.

The secret was Wieden & Kennedy, a young boutique advertising firm in Portland, Oregon, that had once been Nike's sole agency. The shoe company turned over its television work in 1984 to the larger, Los Angeles firm Chiat/Day, but grew disillusioned with the results. After Wieden &

Kennedy sparked industry buzz for their Honda Scooter spots
featuring Lou Reed, Nike looked homeward again. The result was
a series of ads that, far from extolling the specific virtues of Nike
shoes, created a pantheon of surreal, cartoonish characters drawn
from the ranks of entertainment, sports, and even literature:
from Spike Lee's Mars Blackmon to junkie-beat-counterculture
icon William Burroughs to the "Bo Knows" campaign, which
featured the exploits of cross-sport sensation Bo Jackson (and even
guitarist Bo Diddley). There were spots too that painted the company
as the quintessence of hip, taking songs like "Revolution" or John
Lennon's "Instant Karma" and morphing their meanings into an ethos
of personal advancement through training. And then there were the

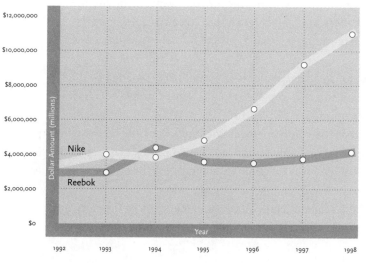

FIGURE 10 *Nike vs. Reebok: Total Revenues, 1992-1998*

Swoosh is the sound you make blowing by somebody. Nike once lagged Reebok in the revenue department, but the 1990s has belonged to the crew from Beaverton, Oregon.
Source: Nike and Reebok company reports

three words that today require no explanation: "Just Do It."

While Reebok's U.B.U. campaign was confusing consumers, Nike's sales doubled from 1987 to 1989. As Randall Rothenberg describes in his book *Where the Suckers Moon*, the kind of advertising Wieden & Kennedy turned out for the company at that time was sparked by the realization Nike had made several years before: it wasn't entirely the shoes. Rothenberg writes:

from ***Where the Suckers Moon***, by Randall Rothenberg (1994):

Their [Wieden & Kennedy's] early work for Nike was virtually all print; the shoe company, which sold $458 million worth of sneakers the year before Wieden & Kennedy took control of its advertising, was leery of television's cost and doubtful of its impact. Nonetheless, the tyro agency soon began adopting the lingo and affectations of larger shops. The ad people stopped talking about meetings, asking instead to make "presentations." At some point, the word "payoff"—meaning the climax or resolution of an advertisement—crept into Dan [Wieden's] vocabulary. The antics reminded some Nike executives of children playing dress-up.

Not that Nike didn't respect Wieden & Kennedy. To the contrary, the company soon came to depend on the agency. Dan especially, for strategic insights and long-term planning. Nike's revenues had increased by a factor of sixteen in the half-decade before Wieden & Kennedy was awarded the account. Now, as valuable members of the company's inner circle, Dan, David and their colleagues believed they would share in its inevitably glowing future—until Nike ran into an army of hopping, skipping and jumping women, all wearing Reebok shoes.

Reebok was Nike's opposite. Where Nike was focused, Reebok was inspirational; where Nike's chief executive, Phil Knight, was educated, directed, and disciplined, Reebok's leader, Paul Fireman, a college dropout and onetime fishing tackle salesman, was mercurial. Fireman managed to quintuple Reebok's running-shoe sales, to $1.5 million, between 1980 and 1981, but fighting against Nike for the feet of runners was a tough business. So in 1981, based purely on observation and hunch, he engineered a change in the company's direction. Fireman was intrigued by aerobics, a heart-pumping exercise fad increasingly popular with young women. He decided to make and sell shoes for that market.

The shoes were the kind that Nike's fanatic runners despised. Reeboks were too narrow for the pounding that runners gave their feet; they were made of soft leather, which was apt to fall apart after a few good bearings on long-distance courses; they were white, which showed the dirt.

But the white footwear was appealing to women who wanted good-looking shoes not only to exercise in but to walk to work in; the soft leather felt like a slipper; and the narrowness flattered women's feet in ways running shoes never could. Reebok's sales curve told the story: from $3.5 million in 1982 to $13 million a year later, virtually without advertising. As the overall American market for branded athletic footwear grew—from $1.8 billion in sales in 1983 to $2.6 billion in 1986—Reebok took the lead, very much at Nike's expense. Reebok's sales nearly quintupled in 1984, to $64 million, and almost quintupled again the next year, to $300 million, then soared again, to $841 million in 1986. Nike's decline was less spectacular, but equivalently steady: from $636 million in 1983, to $625 million in 1985, a year in which the company spent two quarters in the red and saw its profits plummet by 80 percent. In 1986, the company's sales fell to $536 million.

Missing the aerobics book was only a manifestation of Nike's larger problem. A company built by jocks for jocks, where top executives called their no-holds-barred, locker-room-loud management meetings "Buttfaces," Nike had no understanding of or affinity for women. And women were the primary purchasers of shoes in the United States.

The company also failed to understand one of the more compelling explanations for its own, earlier success. It believed its growth was based on its appeal to athletes. It ignored the fact that sales of athletic shoes in the United States closely tracked cultural trends. The running boom, which was, after all, not a permanent change in the American character but a temporary fad exploited by the media, was the real source of Nike's expansion. Instead of hunting for the next sports-as-culture trend, Nike allowed Reebok to find and market it.

Athletic shoe sales, in a word, were a function of fashion—a term Nike did not appreciate or understand. "If you said the word 'fashion' in a Nike meeting," said Peter Moore, the company's design director, "You were a really bad guy. You didn't know what you were talking about."

As Nike's sales fell, its top executives agonized over the reasons, and finally came to an understanding. Reebok had defined itself not by technology or by markets, but in terms of a transcendent image; Nike had merely grafted an image onto its existing rigid orientation around its products and runners. The company forced itself to address a question it had never before asked: *What does our brand stand for?* The answer was uncomfortable:

We are a technology company. But technology is fashion. So we are a fashion company. In order to appeal to the broadest possible market, Nike would have to talk about or present the technology built into its shoes as something fresh.

While that novelty presumably made the shoes better devices for athletic performance, it was not the reason the sneakers lured customers: People were attracted to novelty, the company now reasoned, by the novelty *itself*. Thus, advertising, which from its earliest appearance in modern societies was a means of communicating something new, rose in importance to Nike. Indeed, it became central to Nike's redefinition of its mission.

"For years we thought of ourselves as a production-oriented company, meaning we put all our emphasis on designing and manufacturing the product," Phil Knight said, long after the crisis had passed. "But now we understand that the most important thing we do is market the product. We've come around to saying that Nike is a marketing company, and the product is our most important marketing tool."

But a tool for what? What was Nike *really* marketing if not athletic shoes? The answer was staring the company in the face, embedded in Moore's personality posters. It was selling heroes.

Rob Strasser, the company's marketing director, was the first to advance this odd hypothesis, in a memo explaining the meaning of the posters. "Individual athletes, even more than teams, will be the heroes; symbols more and more of what real people can't do anymore—risk and win," he wrote in 1983. In the middle of its downward spiral, Nike realized that sports heroes, far from being a mere public relations gimmick, might be the very vehicle to drag the company back to health.

These heroes were portrayed in ways that exalted their individualism, however uncomfortable that might be to mainstream America. The false humility with which athletes in older advertisements were imbued, the aw-shucks-I'm-just-like-you attitude they affected, was banished from Nike's posters and ads. John McEnroe, the bad-boy tennis star from Queens, New York, was photographed on New York's 59th Street Bridge, dressed sullenly in black leather à la James Dean. Philadelphia Phillies strikeout king Steve Carlton was shot with a literally blazing baseball in his hand. Moses Malone of basketball's Houston Rockets was depicted in flowing robes reminiscent of his biblical namesake. By individualizing its endorsers, in every element of the company's communications, Nike meant to apotheosize them and implicitly identify itself, their home, as the Olympus of America's 1980s celebrity-worshipping-hero-adoring consumer culture.

The personality posters were central to Nike's great marketing breakthrough. It was no longer marketing its product—shoes—as heroes. It was selling heroes as its product. The purchase of athletic shoes served the consumer like the communion ritual, as transubstantiation. In buying a pair of Nikes, a man or a woman was literally consuming part of a hero, and taking on elements of his (or, later, her) character.

Nike rearranged its business around this transforming idea, signing on as spokesmen, endorsers and contract demigods some of American sports' most individualistic stars, *then* developing product lines around the quirks in their personalities. After the company affiliated with David Robinson and Charles Barkley, two NBA stars whose style of play was aggressive and muscular, it set about developing shoes suited to their tough, confrontational tactics. It dubbed the products the "Force" line. When Scottie Pippen, a basketball player who favored quick moves and high-flying passes and dunks, came on board, Nike developed a more flexible, lighter-weight line of shoes called "Flight."…

ON NEW YEAR'S DAY, 1998, Nike debuted a new ad campaign. Titled "I Can," the spots were meant to put affirmative focus on amateur athletes and represented a pointed shift away from "Just Do It," which the company maintained was not being eliminated altogether. Where "Just Do It" smacked of 1980s aggressiveness and studied disregard for the outcome of one's actions, "I Can" was meant to restore a positive feeling to the company, its reputation (and tagline) battered by criticism over its labor policies in Asia and declining share prices. "At a time when cynicism in sports is at an all-time high," a Nike executive said, "'I Can' is an effort to return to a focus on the positive." But from Alonzo Mourning's comment about working for Nike to the influx of money on the high school and college level, one wondered what role companies such as Nike had to play in the cynicism of sports.

Targeting the Athlete of Tomorrow

Marketing sneakers isn't just about finding the right slogan or crafting the right image. It is also about finding—or even inventing—a market. One of the most famous cases of this was Nike's release of its first "cross-training" shoe in 1987. Before it hit the stores, it is unlikely more than a few people in America would have known what cross-training was, and fewer still would actually have done some of it. In sneaker terms, however, it was the kind of simple idea that sounded good in the showroom and made sense to consumers: light enough for running, yet with the lateral support of a basketball shoe. Versatility was the new watchword, something in between the clunky, overly masculine basketball high-top and the lighter, slightly effete running shoe. The crossing of these boundaries was rather modest compared to what was to follow in the 1990s: myriad hybrids of sandals, "aqua socks," and sneaker-cum-hiking boots that catered to fashion movements as well as a rising interest in "off-road" sports.

Women have long bought the traditional canvas sneaker, but the marketing of the more expensive varieties of athletic shoe to women has only begun recently. As women's sports at various school levels have increased in the last few decades, the shoe companies have jogged in step, releasing new gender-specific models and touting the benefits of women's participation in sports. The shoe companies have a more than casual interest in higher levels of participation: while overall sales of athletic shoes have declined in the last few years after an all-time peak in the early 1990s, the sale of women's sneakers has risen. In the first eight months of 1996, women's shoes outsold men's shoes, 95.1 million pairs to 85.5 million pairs. The women's market is typically less "brand sensitive," meaning a buyer will be more willing to switch to a new brand based on personal taste; in 1993, *Discount Store News* reported, "the top two athletic brands (by all industry accounts Nike and Reebok) were 46 percent of all men's athletic shoe sales; while in women's, the top two accounted for only 30 percent of sales."

Yet that gap is likely to close as more women become involved in organized sports and develop brand allegiances increasingly derived from perceived athletic—rather than strictly fashion—attributes. The debut of the Women's National Basketball Association—itself the result of changing perceptions of professional team sports—has begun to help sell women's basketball shoes, and has had a ripple effect into other sports. Reebok, a sponsor of the WNBA's rival, the American Basketball League, released its first woman-endorsed basketball shoe; Nike, meanwhile, named a shoe after Sheryl Swoopes for her standout Texas Tech college basketball career and was using other women athletes like downhill skier Picabo Street to promote its product.

"Targeting the athlete of tomorrow" begins an ASICS press release announcing the debut of children's running and cross-training shoes. "Recognizing the importance of establishing brand awareness and brand loyalty at an early age," the release continues, "ASICS has made a concerted effort to bring to market products that offer technical products at a value price." With consumers six to eleven making up an increasing athletic shoe segment, according to a recent report compiled by the Athletic Footwear Association, it is no surprise to see ASICS courting the kids market, or Reebok offering a separate "Weebok" line. P.F. Flyers may once have promised that kids could "run faster, jump higher," but today's children's sneakers are extensions (or what the industry calls "take downs") of the adult models, with the same complex-sounding cushioning and stability "systems." Brand recognition, as befits a child-centered consumer marketing explosion that has brought commercials into the school curriculum and fostered products such as the "Ralph Lauren Barbie" and "My First Sony," runs high: sneaker companies enjoy near-universal awareness. Interestingly, though, sneaker ads themselves rarely target children, at the risk of causing "disconnect" with the staple teenage market. As *The Economist* reports, the number of American teenagers is expected to grow from 25 million today to 31 million by 2010. Teenage income, moreover, is predicted to hit $77 billion in 1998—nearly all of it discretionary.

Shoe companies have been criticized for the ever more prevalent role they play in school athletics at various levels. Summer shoe camps have become a fixture of sports, particularly basketball; in a recent NBA draft, seventeen of the first twenty-five players chosen in the draft had attended Nike camps during high school. At the college level, virtually every coach in the Associated Press Top Twenty earns a six-figure salary for being sponsored by a particular company, and universities' entire athletic departments sign deals that cover merchandising, advertising, and product supply. The University of Michigan, for example, signed a six-year, $8 million deal in 1995 with Nike, for which Michigan, in exchange for cash, would provide "logo recognition" in various school sites, promotional appearances by the coaches and other services. At the high school level, sponsorship has grown in part because of a 1982 National Collegiate Athletic Association rule that allowed high school players to sign early "letters of intent" with coaches. The summer leagues, such as the ones started by Nike in 1984, thus emerged as a crucial way to gauge talent. The annual summer championships, as depicted in the documentary film *Hoop Dreams*, are giant talent pools for college scouts. High schools, too, receive direct cash payments from companies; the New York *Daily News* reported in 1996 that the coach of St. Patrick's High School in Elizabeth, New Jersey, was paid twenty thousand dollars by Adidas for his program's endorsement. Sneaker companies even go after individual high school players. Nike, for example, courted Stromile Swift, a junior in Shreveport, Louisiana, offering to outfit his entire team; Swift, as the *Los Angeles Times* reported, agreed to play on a Nike summer all-star team.

Sneaker companies that promote themselves at the high school and college level have two goals in mind: to increase awareness of their brand among athletes (and make further sales among non-athletes who may choose to wear a particular brand in response to an athlete's choice) and to form early relationships with top-caliber players, who they hope will endorse their product if they make it to the NBA. Critics charge that the programs not only increase the commercialization of amateur sports and schools themselves, but create an unequal playing field by rewarding some teams more than others. "Absolutely it [sponsoring high schools] is ruining the parity in high school basketball," Adidas shoe camp head Sonny Vaccaro told the

Los Angeles Times. "But the alternative is to stop. And Nike is not going to do that... and I won't stop." Some see another form of inequity occurring. As the former University of Michigan basketball player Chris Webber said on ESPN in 1997, "The school was selling our jerseys. We're only allowed to get two [cartons of] juice and a pair of gym shoes. The coach had a $300,000 contract with gym shoes." The sneaker companies' currency is cash and shoes, both of which go over well at high schools in poor districts which can ill afford to equip their own teams.

While the sneaker companies may help make a handful of players eventually become wealthy NBA stars, the real social benefit of this sponsorship—in schools where most students can't read at their own grade level—needs to be questioned. In his study of African American culture and sports, *Darwin's Athletes*, John Hoberman notes that "sports themes and styles have soaked into the fabric of African American life, as black identity is athleticized through ubiquitous role models who stimulate wildly unrealistic ambitions in black children—an improbable number of black boys expect to become pro athletes." By throwing money into amateur athletics at various levels, the sneaker companies help perpetuate the myth that athletics can be a lucrative career—replete with sneaker and other endorsement deals—for more than just the talented few.

5

The Finish Line

Tallying the Balance Sheet

"The kid in Singapore, Buenos Aires, or Prague is getting
just about the same exposure to our brand as the kid in Kansas City."
—Walter Schoenfeld, CEO of Vans

Performance Brands

CORPORATE AMERICA consistently draws parallels to sports, a habit that is taken up with particular relish in the athletic shoe industry. Market participants like to refer to the industry as "the game" and the companies as "players." The performance aspects of the shoes are echoed in the financial statements and annual reports of sneaker companies, which intersperse pictures of sports heroes with graphs marking upward slopes of stock prices. Athlete-endorsers are referred to as "on-field assets." "Strategy," "team," "challenge," and the like are used to give the epic quality of a sporting match to the quest for profits and market share.

As befits an industry that pulls in over $7 billion a year in wholesale domestic sales, sneaker companies are closely watched by Wall Street. Firms such as Salomon Brothers produce detailed annual industry surveys that apply specific (even arcane) methodology to forecast a company's performance. Sneakers, like fashion, are dependent on stylistic fads and social trends for their success, and attention must be paid to less tangible factors, such as "brand equity," when gauging a firm's prospects. Salomon Brothers dubs "product equities" such shoes as the Air Jordan or the Converse All-Star, that is, products with a recognizable brand name which can be expected to sell at a particular volume and whose fixed costs for manufacturing and design have already been taken into account. Some shoes, like the Converse All-Star 2000, even possess a "sub-brand equity" or "equity of the actual model name," much the same way the Ford Mustang possesses an identity simply as a "Mustang." One feature of the sneaker market that distinguishes it from the rest of the fashion industry is that certain brands have the value-added benefit of performance features. Thus, Salomon Brothers analyzes the "Fashion Risk Factor" as "1-(Total Product Equity) + (Total Sub-Brand Equity)," which essentially means companies who depend too much on new products and the tides of fashion are riskier investments.

If fixed assets were once the foundation of a firm's strength, for sneakers, as for many other branded products in this "soft goods" stage of capitalism, the logo on the side and the connotations it summons become nearly quantifiable notations on a balance sheet. As Salomon Brothers observed in a 1996 report, "We view product and sub-brand equities as real intangible assets, like goodwill, as real from a dollars-and-cents standpoint as are buildings and machinery. The value of these assets is a function of the consumer's desire to purchase these products for their unique characteristics and quality reputation, and the creator's ability to limit others from copying their design elements and to continue to produce quality product." For many sneaker companies, the brand assumes a larger stature than the company itself or its product. Converse, for example, has consolidated its entire line under one ethos, as described in its 1996 annual report: "Another major step taken in 1996 was the creation of a single new marketing strategy and brand positioning statement that focused our global marketing efforts on the theme, 'Converse All-Star is the American performance brand with authentic sports heritage.' This brand positioning builds on the rich, sports heritage of Converse and the success and consumer recognition of the Converse All-Star brand."

One consequence of this careful promotion of brand equity and lifestyle marketing has been a dramatic rise in the sale of branded athletic apparel by the shoe companies. For the top three companies in 1996, apparel commands an increasingly large share of their business: for Nike, apparel represented 25 percent of sales and was growing 69 percent a year; for Reebok, 19 percent of sales and rising 26 percent a year; for Fila, 35 percent of sales and growing 52 percent a year. Shoe companies have begun to make products such as sunglasses and sports equipment (Nike, for example, sells "running eyewear" for $145 and the ACG Karst 25 "panel-loading mountaineering-style pack" for eighty dollars).

Another reason brand has become so important in the sneaker industry is that brand equity, logo, and advertising are what move the shoe across borders, and international sales are playing a larger and larger role in sneaker company fortunes. According to company reports, over one-third of Nike's total 1996 revenues (approximately $2.5 billion) came from abroad; other companies reported similar results proportionally. Despite being a truly multinational shoe, Nike for one enjoys an all-American image, which is bolstered by endorsements from top U.S. athletes. The swoosh, moreover, translates easily. Although Nike has stated it wants half of its sales to come from abroad by the year 2000, it has faced resistance cracking the world soccer market, for decades sewn up by Puma and Adidas (who maintain close ties to soccer's international governing body). Nike signed "hard lads" such as Manchester United's star Eric Cantona and Brazilian legend Ronaldo, and aired cheeky and controversial ads (one spot showed Satan's henchmen playing with a group of European soccer stars), but the very same big-spending rebel status that played so well in the U.S. has ruffled feathers abroad. In 1997, it was alleged that Nike tried to stop Ronaldo from changing teams since the company didn't want to see the star striker wearing a jersey with another logo.

Still, Nike now dominates markets like Britain, where an estimated £850 million worth of shoes were sold in 1996; in contrast to 1988, when Nike had about 10 percent of a £340 million market, behind Reebok at 12 percent and leader Hi-Tec at 25 percent. In China, where Nike has begun trying to sell the shoes it once only made there, the company has toned down its "rebel" image. To try and make inroads into a market dominated by cheap canvas and plastic sneakers and Chinese athletic brands such as Li Ning and Kang Wei, Nike has discarded its traditional U.S. endorsers in favor of local talent, such as basketball star Hu Weidong.

Not just big companies with superstar endorsers have been adopted as tokens of Americanness abroad. Vans, for example, which followed the Nike model of overseas production, has also begun reaching out to international markets. Sales to global accounts, the *Los Angeles Times* reported, jumped 103.5 percent from fiscal 1995 to fiscal 1996. As Vans' CEO, Walter Schoenfeld, told the *Wall Street Journal*, "The kid in Singapore, Buenos Aires or Prague is getting just about the same exposure to our brand as the kid in Kansas City. We're really just kicking it off overseas." (See Figure 11, page 146)

Like some girls ached for their first brassiere, I pined for a pair of cleats. It's not that our field hockey pitch was so smooth and sleek that I really needed them for traction—indeed, the piece of Illinois ground assigned to Highland Park High School's girls' team was rarely mowed and not even flat—but I knew that those plastic protrusions underfoot would proclaim I was a serious athlete. I could see myself loping to practice on lumpy soles, my legs bowing out over their uneven but certain purchase on the earth.

Truth is, my legs bowed anyway, even in my everyday flats, my Converse All-Stars. And though I was not as emphatic as my best friend Fran, whose annual new pair of All-Stars were *always* black high-tops, I had well understood the fashion fundamentals drummed into every teenaged female: Shoes make the outfit. And the out*cast*. Risking ridicule, we eschewed femmy pointy-toed Keds and sauntered with pre-conscious defiance in sneakers that could be bought only in the boys' department. Other girls rebelled, they thought, by primping in fuck-me pumps. Our Converse, and more so the cleats we coveted, said fuck *you*.

Miraculously, I got a pair. One August night, just before the new practice season would begin, I blew out candles and my mother handed me a card that concluded: "When it comes to ways of dressing we have such different views / Still, for your 15th birthday, you get a pair of hockey shoes." The next day we made the pilgrimage to the sporting goods store, where I was giddily fitted for a pair of black leather Adidas

by a salesman who kept smirking at his colleague in the storeroom. I noticed; my mom pretended not to. As soon as we got into the car, I took the fragrant shoes from the box and fingered their jagged white stripes as feverishly as any fetishist ever stroked a set of T-straps.

Twenty-five years later—and nearly as many years after Title IX legislated equal spending on men's and women's athletics, among other things, at state-funded colleges—the only folks taking unabashed pleasure in the feminist frisson of athletic footwear are the marketing strategists at the big sports shoe companies. It's a little hard to stomach. Even as more girls join teams, more women work out, and more elite athletes gain the adulation—and endorsement contracts—once reserved for men, their coaches and promoters, and with rare exception the athletes themselves, strain ever more strenuously to insist that girl jocks aren't butch.

Yes, yes. It's grand that so many more girls are playing sports nowadays. It's thrilling that cleats come in girls' sizes. And I can't even imagine how it would have felt to plaster Mia Hamm pix on my wall instead of Gale Sayres. Yet, my jock heart cries, don't let them make sports normal, unthreatening, as hetero as ballet. Not until they've run some wind-sprints in my shoes.

from **The Best Seat in the House**
by Spike Lee (1997):

A pair of high-top Converse Chuck Taylor All-Stars cost eight bucks [in the 1960s]. I normally wore P.F. Flyers or Keds, but I begged my parents for my first pair of Cons. Only little kids wore those sissy P.F. Flyers or Keds. I was an athlete and I needed to wear what the other athletes wore. There is something about a new pair of sneakers that makes a boy feel he can run faster and jump higher, and they also made a fashion statement not so different from how it is today, although there is much more to covet in this day and time. But back then the most coveted legitimizing agent for the discerning youth was white high-top canvas Chuck Taylor All-Stars. The Knicks wore them. So did the Lakers. Everybody did. They were the only right thing to wear. If you wanted to get fancy, you'd adorn them with colorful shoelaces. I vividly recall getting my first pair of Chucks and wearing them proudly as all my friends' eyes sought out their glory.

Learning from Nike Town

BUYING A NEW PAIR OF SNEAKERS is a time-honored and nearly universal adolescent ritual (as the accompanying literary excerpts reveal). But the days when a new pair of tennis shoes would be purchased at a local shoe merchant or sporting goods store have mostly vanished; small, mall-based chains such as Athlete's Foot, where I remember buying my first pair of Nikes, are being eclipsed by even larger entities. Today, "big box" retail is the norm—either

FIGURE 11 *U.S. Sales vs. Global Sales: Top Ten Companies, 1996*

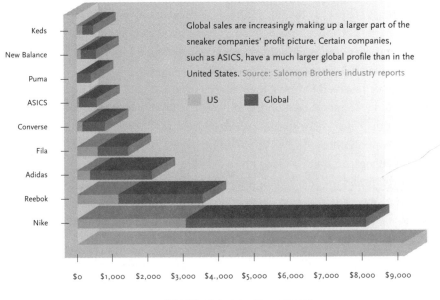

Global sales are increasingly making up a larger part of the sneaker companies' profit picture. Certain companies, such as ASICS, have a much larger global profile than in the United States. Source: Salomon Brothers industry reports

US Global

Keds
New Balance
Puma
ASICS
Converse
Fila
Adidas
Reebok
Nike

$0 $1,000 $2,000 $3,000 $4.,000 $5,000 $6,000 $7,000 $8,000 $9,000

SALES (wholesale in millions, estimated)

mass discounters or flashy specialty warehouses—as it is with home improvement centers or bookselling superstores. Foot Locker, one of the first sneaker specialty stores (the chain had ninety-eight stores in the summer of 1979), is still the industry leader, with some 1,625 stores worldwide, but in the last few years upstarts such as The Sports Authority, Sneaker Stadium, and Champs have made inroads. (See Figure 12) The market is hardly limited to these outlets, however; for women's athletic shoes, sports footwear chain stores tallied 33.8 percent of sales in 1997, according to *Footwear News*, department stores accounted for 26.7 percent, while shoe stores took a 12.2 percent share and mass discounters took most of the rest with 11.2 percent.

Selling sneakers is a potentially lucrative yet risky business. A successful shoe will fly off the shelves, often leaving a retailer under-stocked; while a much-hyped shoe, such as Nike's Air Penny, can prove a bust and require deep discounting. The sneaker companies try to limit their exposure to this risk by "allocating" small initial shipments to help build a rising demand curve, as well as by occasionally pruning the number of retailers selling its product; Nike has even taken the step of instituting a "futures program" in which retailers receive discounts for agreeing to buy a certain volume of shoes in advance. "Retailers get an early sense of what we think is a hot shoe," a Nike spokesman told *Footwear News*. "We can predict better and don't over-manufacture and (in turn) have to discount and close out." Nike, Reebok, and similar companies zealously guard the integrity of their brand, selling only to select retailers (Nike, for example, gave a cool reception early on to the New Jersey-based

Sneaker Stadium, which gave the impression of being a "price-driven" retailer—one that would mark down Nike product and thus tarnish its image) and in general trying to avoid having their product sit next to "off-brand" products on a cluttered discount-store shelf. The rise and fall of Puma in the United States in the 1970s is considered an object lesson: "Mass merchants used up the name," a retailer told *Footwear News* in 1982, "to the point where it no longer had value." The extreme end of this attempt to control the market has led to several price-fixing cases filed against a number of athletic shoe companies (including

FIGURE 12 *Top Ten Sporting Goods Retailers, 1996*

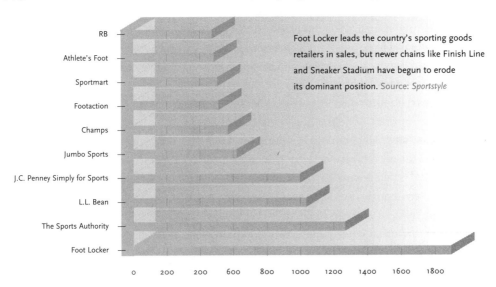

Foot Locker leads the country's sporting goods retailers in sales, but newer chains like Finish Line and Sneaker Stadium have begun to erode its dominant position. Source: *Sportstyle*

SALES (in millions)

Reebok and New Balance) by the Federal Trade Commission.

In the last few years, the trend in selling athletic shoes has been to create "entertainment retail" establishments, where shoes, apparel, and, sometimes, athletic equipment are sold in an environment filled with sports trappings. These stores can be up to ten times the size of a normal mall specialty store, and inside their confines "brand boutiques," which focus on one particular company's product, are set up. Nike has taken this a giant step further by creating Nike Towns, massive centers of "inspirational sports retail" that contain some sixty thousand square feet of merchandise, memorabilia, and even an "interactive display" in which shoppers can touch the various air bags found in different shoe cushionings. The first store opened in Portland in 1990, but the company has since added outlets in Chicago, New York, and other cities. Nike's Gordon Thompson, quoted in *Architectural Record*, described the store's function as something more profound than selling sneakers: "We need Nike Town stores to carry the Nike story. We're using architecture as a communication device for a brand."

Brands *are* communication devices of sorts, so it's striking to see another medium, such as architecture, interpreting the swoosh. Walking through a Nike Town store is like entering a Nike commercial: one is surrounded by giant images of athletes, bombarded with wall text describing the company ethos, enveloped by music and light. It feels like a factory, less for products than a brand. Workers patrol the floor and keep the product moving along, the output is stacked neatly, ready for shipment, and the raw materials— the logos, athletic images, and advertising slogans—are piled everywhere, ready to be processed. Even the amped-up music and sports sound effects that resonate everywhere are akin to the hum of machinery. As is appropriate for a factory of the brand, which focuses on the image and aura of the product, there are no displays dedicated to the assembly of Nike shoes, or even any hint where they come from: they would seem, by dint of the wall text, to come straight from the mind of Nike design or to have been born on some 100-meter track in Oregon (a 1997 Nike ad for "CEO Jordan" hinted at this mystery when it showed Jordan "inspecting" his new line of shoes, putting an "inspected by no. 23" tag in each—yet who really could summon a mental picture of who inspected the shoes?). The New York Nike Town plays with this fiction even further, using an architectural theme that blends a "classic New York school gymnasium" with a "futuristic retail structure." Nike is in essence reinserting itself into a history in which it didn't exist, an era before companies paid tens of millions of dollars to athletes to wear its shoes, sponsored high school basketball camps, or sold sneakers at several times the cost of a pair of blue jeans.

In Chicago, it is easy to spot Nike Town, even with the competing enticements of what civic boosters call the "Magnificent Mile." The store's entrance is marked by a trio of athletes set in bronze relief, and groups of tourists and local teenagers are usually clustered in front of this "sports retail theater" (as the press kit describes it), which happens to be Chicago's "top retail tourist attraction." At a time when spartan wholesale clubs and strip malls rule the American consumer sensibility, Nike Town bristles with novelty. It is, in the developer's phrase, "packed with program," an aspiring mixed-use mecca: museum, art gallery, Pantheon, fashion boutique, cathedral, environment, entertainment, and, finally, store. But essentially it is a live, interactive commercial celebrating Nike's market share. Like the company's increasingly abstract television spots, Nike Town tells consumers that Nike is so ingrained in our culture that its image makers can transcend the quotidian act of selling and move on to more interesting things.

In my first visit to Nike Town in Chicago, I was immediately greeted by a display recounting the history of Nike: how this multimillion dollar industry was born during one fateful breakfast, in which Bill Bowerman saw in his waffle iron the stuff of championship athletic footwear. He quickly turned that epiphany into his trademarked Waffle Outsole. Nike Town's mythico-historical alcove is the locus of the entire store, the timeless tale of invention and American entrepreneurial spirit. Everything that follows comes of this encounter with a kitchen appliance.

The lobby opens into a vast three-tiered atrium, where ambient New Age sounds fill the air and mountain bikes bearing Nike-clad chalk-colored effigies hang from the ceiling (looking suspiciously like works by George Segal). Giant pneumatic tubes run vertically along the sides, whisking shoes and other products silently up and down from the unseen storage center to the pavilion in need. Behind a wall of aqua socks and Nike sandals a school of tropical fish drifts idly by, as people move in more closely to gauge their authenticity.

Nike Town, I soon discovered, is filled with aggressively documented displays, ranging from a design schematic of Nike Town Chicago (from which we learn that the "building itself and every shoe, shirt, sock, hat or bag in it comes from the mind of Nike design") to a pair of boots worn by Batman in the Tim Burton film (they are modeled on Air Jordan shoes, we learn) and are yet another example of the Nike designer Tinker Hatfield's "cross-inspirational thinking." In the arc-shaped Nike Theater, shoppers watch their favorite Nike commercials, as well as a Nike video that depicts children running through inner-city landscapes, major league baseball players, and young children swimming in the ocean, all united by the Nike Swoosh.

A giant banner, visible from the building's third tier, hints at a new genre: marketing poetry. "You are born," it begins, "And oh, how you wail / Your first breath is a scream / Not timid or low, but selfish and shattering, with all the force of waiting nine months underwater / The rest of your life an announcement / Just Do It." Not far away is the work of a more famous poet. On the wall of a reproduced basketball court is a towering mural of His Airness, Michael Jordan, soaring through the sky in his characteristic pose, one arm extended high, ready for the trademark dunk, tongue lolling slightly, elevating and *then* deciding, emboldened by, of all things, the words of William Blake: "No bird soars too high / If he soars with his own wing." Michael Jordan and William Blake! Whose imagination would not be enraptured by this artistic and athletic alley-oop? No longer will I be able to read the famous line in Blake's "Milton"—"And did those feet in Ancient time / Walk upon England's mountains green"—

without wondering whether those feet were wearing Nikes. Could it have been the Air Current RWs in the white and light-thistle color scheme? Or was it the white-and-black-purple slate Air Trainer Accel Lows? And what was Blake really thinking when he penned those lines? Was it the shoes, William?

I approached a woman taking notes, who turned out to be an interior design student. She raved, with self-confessed bias, of how Nike Town's space "replicated itself" and how the various pavilions, representing different environments (and sports) radiate outward from the Town Square, itself decorated with "actual manhole covers." Nike Town, she said excitedly, is a "city within a city." Here, I thought, was the metropolis of the future, a self-contained biosphere of consumption, stripped of the four elements and replaced with MIDI and light effects, the products themselves part of the enveloping sensorium, not to be bought so much as experienced.

Nike Town, billed as the "future of retailing," is actually a return to the heyday of American mass retailing. More than a futuristic marvel, Nike Town is a technologically upgraded version of the turn-of-the-century department stores that the historian William Leach has called "mazes of glittering crystal," and a perfect example of how the cultural sea changes those earlier stores augured have become so entrenched in American life.

from **Dandelion Wine,**
by Ray Bradbury (1956):

One moment, the door to Sanderson's Shoe Emporium was empty. The next, Douglas Spaulding stood clumsily there, staring down at his leather shoes as if these heavy things could not be pulled up out of the cement. The thunder had stopped when his shoes stopped. Now, with painful slowness, daring to look only at the money in his cupped hand, Douglas moved out of the bright sunlight of Saturday noon. He made careful stacks of nickels, dimes, and quarters on the counter, like someone playing chess, and worried if the next move carried him out into sun or deep into shadow.

"Don't say a word!" said Mr. Sanderson.

Douglas froze.

"First, I know just what you want to buy," said Mr. Sanderson. "Second, I see you every afternoon at my window; you think I don't see? You're wrong. Third, to give it its full name, you want the Royal Crown Creme-Sponge Para Litefoot Tennis Shoes:

153

'LIKE MENTHOL ON YOUR FEET!' Fourth, you want credit."

"No!" cried Douglas, breathing hard, as if he's run all night in his dreams. "I got something better than credit to offer!" he gasped. "Before I tell, Mr. Sanderson, you got to do me one small favor. Can you remember when was the last time you yourself wore a pair of Litefoot sneakers, sir?" Mr. Sanderson's face darkened. "Oh, ten, twenty, say, thirty years ago. Why...?"

"Mr. Sanderson, don't you think you owed it to your customers, sir, to at least try the tennis shoes you sell, for just one minute, so you know how they feel? People forget if they don't keep testing things. United Cigar Store man smokes cigars, don't he? Candy-store man samples his own stuff, I should think. So..."

"You may have noticed," said the old man, "I'm wearing shoes."

"But not sneakers, sir! How you going to sell sneakers unless you can rave about them and how you going to rave about them unless you know them?"

Advertising no longer shocks; indeed, it is welcomed as culture, to be discussed only in terms of the ad's quality. For shoppers, a visit to a discount outlet is a reminder that they are trying to save money. At Nike Town, the products are *never* on sale, so Nike must convince buyers that they are buying more than simply products when they willingly part with $450 for a complete running outfit. What they are buying is a lifestyle, Nike's "total body conditioning," in which physical fitness acquires a tone of religious zeal, driven home by mantras and slogans. Nike's advertising campaigns resemble the rhetoric of the "mind cure" groups of early twentieth-century American culture: post-Protestant religious sects that combined healthy-minded, positive thinking with consumerism, as a parallel means to moral uplift. "All you desire is YOURS NOW" the mind cure advocates wrote, a bit of motivational verse worthy of Nike's "Just Do It."

What is ultimately fascinating about Nike Town is the way in which corporate consumer capitalism has absorbed and seemingly replaced so many other spheres of culture. We can see in Nike Town the minute architectural touches of a Gaudí and the ambitious, all-encompassing design aesthetic of the Bauhaus; we can read verses of poetry and thrall to the achievements of our greatest Nike-endorsing athletes.

But do not be fooled. Nike marketing knows better. "Every detail," as a Nike Town brochure reminds us, "whether it screams or whispers, says Nike. Nothing but Nike."

Rubber Soul

While sneakers currently adorn a majority of the country's feet, that has been so only for a fraction of sneaker history. The market has proven to be full of lightning-fast starts and dramatic routs; like the shoes, it has proven incredibly resilient, and as each successive trend or fashion has waned, another has risen to take its place. The running craze gave way to aerobics, a slip in basketball shoes was countered by a rise in the "cross-trainer," and when the aerobics shoe (as fashion anyway) tanked out, simple white canvas sneakers made a comeback. As the generation that made running shoes a staple has aged, walking has arisen as a pursuit with its own lifestyle magazines and equipment.

Since athletic shoes have always evolved in step with technological innovations, it remains an open question what the shoes of the next millennium will look like. The dictates

Mr. Sanderson backed off a little distance from the boy's fever, one hand to his chin. "Well..."

"Mr. Sanderson," said Douglas, "you sell me something and I'll sell you something just as valuable."

"Is it absolutely necessary to the sale that I put on a pair of sneakers, boy?" said the old man.

"I sure wish you could, sir!"

The old man sighed. A minute earlier, seated panting quietly, he laced the tennis shoes to his long narrow feet. They looked detached and alien down there next to the dark cuffs of his business suit. Mr. Sanderson stood up.

"How do they *feel*?" asked the boy.

"How do they feel, he asks; they feel fine." He started to sit down.

"Please!" Douglas held out his hand. "Mr. Sanderson, now could you kind of rock back and forth a little, sponge around, bounce kind of, while I tell you the rest? It's this: I give you my money, you give me the shoes, I owe you a dollar. But, Mr. Sanderson, *but*—soon as I get those shoes on, you know what *happens*?"

"What?"

"Bang! I deliver your packages, pick up packages, bring you coffee, burn your trash, run to the post office, telegraph office, library! You'll see twelve of me in and out, in and out, every minute. Feel those shoes, Mr. Sanderson, *feel* how fast they'd take me? All those springs inside? Feel all the running inside? Feel how they kind of grab hold and can't let you alone and don't like you just *standing* there? Feel how quick I'd be doing things you'd rather not bother with? You stay in the nice cool store while I'm jumping all around town! But it's not me really, it's the shoes. They're going like mad down alleys, cutting corners, and back! There they go!"

Mr. Sanderson stood amazed with the rush of words. When the words got going the flow carried him; he began to sink deep in the shoes, to flex his toes; limber his arches, test his ankles. He rocked softly, secretly, back and forth in a small breeze from the open door. The tennis shoes silently hushed themselves deep in the carpet,

of fashion, moreover, may render the sneaker stylistically obsolete. In the past few years, driven in part by fashion trends and a move toward more relaxed office attire, the "brown shoe," as it is known in the industry, has made a comeback against the predominant "white shoe." In 1997, the *Wall Street Journal* reported that stock analysts were predicting hard times ahead for chains such as Foot Locker and Footaction, due in part to overexpansion and in part to a turn in youth spending away from athletic shoes and toward heavy industrial-inspired boots by Caterpillar and other brands. Again, it was the "urban" market that first tipped off the street: "Inner-city guys in New York City wore boots all summer long," a Smith Barney analyst told the *Wall Street Journal*.

The market's woes in 1997 were exacerbated by the financial crises sweeping Asia. Currency devaluations in countries such as Thailand, where Nike and others have developed nascent consumer markets—not just production sites—left consumers with less disposable income to spend on high-priced sneakers. Nike even planned an advertising campaign designed to soothe the national consuming consciousness of Thailand, a way of saying "we feel your pain." And to keep sales humming along, the currency devaluations did make it cheaper for U.S. companies to produce sneakers in Asia, but they were finding a tighter market back home, at least for certain product categories. "The Answer," the highly awaited follow-up to the Allen Iverson-endorsed Reebok sneaker "The Question," proved a bust at $120 a pair. The shares of Reebok, as well as several other companies, had hit a 52-week low. New York City stores were selling Vans and other overstocked pairs at two for one. The market was glutted.

Some took the falloff in sales as a sign that American consumers had finally come to their senses. "It is undeniable that, in this era of pre-fabricated image, the shoe is the centerpiece of the urban hip-hop look," an editorialist assessing the failure of the Iverson shoe wrote in the Cleveland *Plain Dealer*. "The Big Sneaker exploitation appears to have reached its zenith, however, and may be on the wane." As had happened before, however, the writer's disgruntlement with the industry or the product seemed to extend only to "urban" youths and basketball shoes. It was presumably acceptable for a suburban white-collar worker to spend $110 on a running shoe but not acceptable for a black teenager to spend the same on a basketball shoe. The latter, it was decided, was a duped follower of fashion while the former was a serious athlete

sank as in a jungle grass, in loam and resilient clay. He gave one solemn bounce of his heels in the yeasty dough, in the yielding and welcoming earth. Emotions hurried over his face as if many colored lights had been switched on and off. His mouth hung silently open. Slowly he gentled and rocked himself to a halt, and the boy's face faded and they stood there looking at each other in a tremendous and natural silence.

 157

A few people drifted by on the sidewalk outside, in the hot sun.

Still the man and boy stood there, the boy glowing, the man with revelation in his face.

"Boy," said the old man at last, "in five years, how would you like a job selling shoes in this emporium?"

"Gosh, thanks, Mr. Sanderson, but I don't know what I'm going to be yet."

"Anything you want to be son," said the old man, "you'll be. No one will ever stop you."

The old man walked lightly across the store to the wall of ten thousand boxes, came back with some shoes for the boy, and wrote *up a list on some paper while the boy was lacing the shoes on his feet and then standing there, waiting. The old man held out his list. "A dozen things you got to do for me this afternoon. Finish them, we're even Stephen, and you're fired."*

"Thanks, Mr. Sanderson!"

Douglas bounded away.

"Stop!" cried the old man.

Douglas pulled up and turned. Mr. Sanderson leaned forward.

"How do they feel?"

The boy looked down at his feet deep in the rivers, in the fields of wheat, in the wind that already was rushing him out of the town. He looked up at the old man, his eyes burning, his mouth moving, but no sound came out.

"Antelopes?" said the old man, looking from the boys face to his shoes. "Gazelles?"

The boy thought about it, hesitated, and nodded a quick nod. Almost immediately he vanished. He just spun about with a whisper and went off. The door stood empty. The sound of the tennis shoes faded in the jungle heat.

focused only on function. But how much difference was there between the ads that equated running shoes with personal achievement or corporate ladder-climbing and the ads for basketball shoes that equated the product with earning respect on the court and on the streets? Both were tokens in some kind of personal transformation, even if they occurred in radically different worlds. One consistently heard how foolish it was to spend money on high-priced sneakers, but rarely did one hear of the folly of buying a heavily marked-up Ralph Lauren blazer, an expensive vodka, a luxury sedan, or any other product purchased more for the sake of establishing a level of prestige or standing (also a "prefabricated image") than for its actual functional attributes.

How did the sneaker ever reach the point where it could be the subject of indignant editorials? It had risen in the popular estimation thanks to the fitness movement of the 1970s, but it was not simply a matter of athletics: there is no reason people could not simply have continued running and playing basketball in the same relatively simple and inexpensive shoes they had in the 1960s. Several other things had to happen. First, consumers had to believe that there was a technology to athletic shoes and that better shoes would make them a better athlete. Second, the marketing of athletic superstars was a crucial "value-added" component of sneakers: consumers wouldn't spend a lot for just any sneaker, but to wear the same shoe as their favorite athlete, one was willing to spend a premium. Third, fashion had to change. Just as the easing of school dress codes in the 1950s had enabled the first sneaker boom among children, the easing of societal dress codes over the last several decades made it possible to wear sneakers to work, to restaurants, to church. They were comfortable, in most cases relatively inexpensive, and by wearing them—as by wearing athletic jerseys, track suits, or baseball caps—one was proclaiming allegiance not to just a brand or a favorite team, but to an athletic sensibility.

FIGURE 13 *Top Athletic Shoe Companies by U.S. Sales, 1992–96*

In the Land of the Giants. Nike and Reebok are the twin towers of the sneaker business, while a handful of companies strive to break out of their niche and gain the third position.

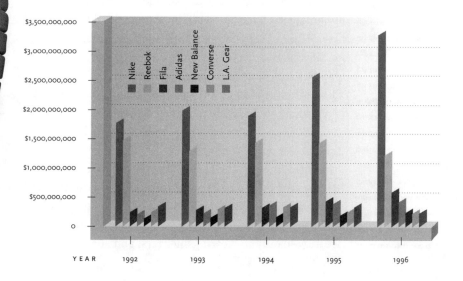

from
The White Boy Shuffle
by Paul Beatty (1996):

Buying basketball shoes was much harder than I thought. Unlike the skate shop, where there are only three different brands and maybe ten styles to choose from, Tennies from Heaven was the footwear equivalent of an automobile showroom. A sneaker emporium where the walls were lined with hundreds of shoes and the sales-men dressed in silk sweatsuits patrolled the floor, handing out brochures, shaking hands, and checking credit ratings. The basketball section took up the entire third floor. An $80 sneaker caught my eye and I hefted it in my hand as if its weight might tell something about its quality. I was about to call for a salesperson when I heard Scoby snickering behind my back and singing, "Buddies, they cost a dollar ninety-nine. Buddies, they make your feet feel fine." I put the shoe down and Nicholas pushed me through the sliding glass door into an area

Sneakers are the emblematic product of the late 20th century. In their 19th-century invention they seemed derived from sailing ships, all white canvas with their "plimsoll" line and solid rubber hull skidding across the pavement; as this annum closed they were more akin to space shuttles, with breathable Kevlar, soles packed with rigidly geometric "pods" and other boosters, a gently sloping aerodynamic exterior daubed in soft metallic tints. They combine fashion and function, athletics and entertainment, rapidly changing technology and planned obsolescence (or, in their original and enduring incantation, classic lines and simple American pragmatism). They are worn by young and old, from Nike's "Baby Swoosh Crib Shoe" for infants, to the sneakers doctors recommend to elderly patients suffering from knee problems and other ailments. Like blue jeans, they have become part of a global outfit, but with the added dimension of Michael Jordan and other marketable commodities they have a much wider reach (although, as one analyst noted in 1997, the financial woes suffered by the Levi's company—due in part to a move away from wearing jeans—were linked to that year's slippage in athletic shoe sales: "there is a very high correlation between wearing jeans and wearing sneakers, and sneakers don't go well with twill pants" the analyst told the *Los Angeles Times*). New retro reissues of classic sneakers win new adherents, while diehard customers spend lavishly to acquire original models through vintage clothing stores and other outlets. They are inexpensive to produce, and the profit margin can be high if one is able to read the winds of fashion correctly.

Their high-tech appearance belies a system of production that has hardly changed from a century before; while the stitchers are drawn from villages in Indonesia and Vietnam, the design, advertising, and other "knowledge" jobs, meanwhile, are based in the United States.

What the sneaker companies ultimately produce is consumers, not sneakers; to produce consumers they create image, entertainment, fashion, and lifestyle. In 1997, the media conglomerate Time Warner announced that it too was entering the sneaker business with WB Sport, which would produce Shaquille O'Neal-endorsed, Reebok-licensed low-end sneakers (Reebok would continue to produce a more expensive variety). Cognizant of the $1 billion in merchandise sold (at Warner Bros. Studio stores and elsewhere) for the Michael Jordan vehicle *Space Jam*, a Time Warner official told *Entertainment Weekly*, "the line between athletes and [entertainment] stars has blurred." Indeed,

of the store called the Proving Grounds—a section of the store where state-of-the-art, more expensive models were on display. Before the staff allowed me to try on any shoes, I had to sign a release stating that if my new sneakers were forcibly removed from my feet and the crime received any media attention, I would blame the theft on the current administration and not on niche marketing.

Even with all the paperwork, I could only try on one shoe at a time, since I wasn't accompanied by a bonded legal guardian or a basketball coach. Whenever I slipped my foot into a new shoe I'd hobble over to the mirror like Tiny Tim Cratchit and blink really fast, trying to create an optical illusion so I could imagine what wearing both sneakers at the same time would look like. After some eyestrain, I managed to convince the guy to let me try a different shoe on each foot and teetered over to Nicholas to ask his opinions. He vetoed the sporty Barbarian on my left foot because they were sewn by eight-year-old Sri Lankans who worked in open-air factories, received no lunch breaks, and were paid in candy bars. The Air Idi Amin Fire Walker on my right foot, a colorful suede high-top, designed to look like a traditional African mask, was nixed because while the shoes performed well on asphalt, they tended to slip on gym floors, and besides, the kids chanted *"Coup d'état, coup d'état!"* at anyone who wore them. Nick suggested the high-tech Adidas Forum II's, an outrageously expensive pair of plain white basketball shoes, computer-designed for maximum support, something called, "wearability," and exactly like the pair he was wearing. The salesperson, smelling commission, closed the deal with a spiel about French cowhide hand-sewn with French thread by French seamstresses who were paid by French entrepreneurs who donated a percentage of every shoe sold to help build basketball courts

WB Sport's trademarked catchphrase was "Sports Is Entertainment." A deal was also struck between Rupert Murdoch's Fox Network and Regency Productions, a film company and large Puma shareholder; the deal was predicted to result in "plenty of Puma product placement in Fox films."

The line between athletes and entertainment had, of course, already been blurred, and sneakers went along for the ride. But where the shoe companies had cultivated the entertainment aspect of athletes to help sell shoes, now the media companies were utilizing the entertainment aspect of athletes to help sell movies, video games, and branded merchandise of dizzying proportion, including, finally, sneakers. It was a logical progression in an evolving economy in which it was not the product which was so important, but what the product said, either literally or figuratively. There was precedent for this in the world of sneakers: in 1934, for example, the Sears catalogue listed "Mickey Mouse White Canvas Shoes." The Time Warner announcement and similar developments portend a much more vertically and horizontally integrated arrangement; hypothetically, the company can sell the sneakers that appeared in one of its own films in its own stores.

Despite vulcanization, side ventilating eyelets, the Waffle sole or other technical innovations in the sneaker century, the end product is essentially the same now as it has always been: a lightweight shoe with a rubber sole (real or synthetic) intended for athletics or casual wear. Sneakers themselves changed less than did the culture around them. Whether sneakers will ever reach the sales plateau they did in the early 1990s, or whether they will continue to be the leading shoe sold in America, is open to speculation.

For the time being, however, athletic shoes of all stripes hold sway as fin-de-siècle footwear. The basic canvas sneakers of yesterday are pure, simply totems of carefree leisure and low-cost functionality and a nostalgic gesture toward dimly remembered summer lawns and sidewalk hopscotch. The evolving athletic shoes point toward the future. The marketing behind them, filled with faith in technology and a regenerative quest for constant self-improvement, speaks to the confidence of science over nature and an ever-increasing athletic capacity of the human body (aided by technology). It also hints at a forestalling of mortality: there is no finish line.

in ghettos throughout the world. I wanted to comment on how building more basketball courts just created a demand for more sneakers, but instead gimped around the store, hopped up and down on one foot, and put one hundred and seventy-five dollars on the counter. The salesman smiled and handed me the other shoe and the carbon copy of the release form.

Source Notes

I HAVE RELIED on a wide number of interviews, articles, television and radio programs, original documents, and promotional materials in writing this book. Articles that are quoted in the text are listed below in the order in which they appear. I have interviewed a number of persons at various athletic shoe companies and other segments of the industry; some of these are quoted, others are not. Given the extremely competitive nature of the industry, employees are reluctant to give out any information or numbers that may prove useful to another sneaker company.

I have relied particularly heavily on a number of trade publications that cover the shoe and sport industries, *Footwear News* and *Sportstyle* in particular, as well as *Sporting Goods Intelligence*. Trade groups such as the Sporting Goods Marketing Association and Footwear Industries of America tabulate key statistics in the industry, as do annual reports from those athletic shoe companies that are publicly held. I have also been benefited by the work of former Salomon Brothers analyst Brett Barakett, who keeps a close watch on the industry. Quotes from sneaker advertisements, unless otherwise noted, are taken from the promotional material itself.

The welfare of workers in the Asian shoe factories has been well documented, if under-publicized, by groups such as Community Aid Abroad, Global Exchange, Press for Change, Vietnam Labor Watch, and others. These groups publish reports on the World Wide Web and through newsletters.

Chapter One

Fisher, Ian, "A New Jordan Sneaker Inspires a Frenetic Run," *The New York Times*, July 4, 1996.

Goldman, Steven L., Nagel, Roger N., and Preiss, Kenneth, "Why Seiko Has 3,000 Watch Styles," *The New York Times*, October 9, 1994.

Barakett, Brett, "The Athletic Footwear and Apparel Industry," Salomon Brothers report, December 3, 1996.

"The Nike Economy," *Far Eastern Economic Review*, September 5, 1996.

Barber, Benjamin, *Jihad vs. McWorld* (New York: Times Books, 1995).

Blackford, Mansel G., and Kerr, K. Austin, *B.F. Goodrich: Tradition and Transformation, 1870-1995* (Columbus: Ohio State University Press, 1996).

"Trainers, sneakers, and shoes: In the Vanguard," *The Economist*, June 7, 1997.

Tenner, Edward, *Why Things Bite Back: Technology and the Revenge of Unintended Consequences* (New York: Alfred A. Knopf, 1996).

Cox, James A., "Being snuck up on by 'sneaker chic'" *Smithsonian*, January, 1986.

Hyde, Nina S. "They've Got Heart, They've Got Sole; The Aura of Sneakers," *Washington Post*, August 18, 1978.

Cheskin, Melvyn P., *The Complete Handbook of Athletic Footwear* (New York: Fairchild Publications, 1987).

Elliot Gorn and Warren Goldstein, *A Brief History of American Sports* (New York: Hill and Wang, 1993).

"Revolution," *The New Yorker*, May 12, 1962.

"The jogging-shoe race heats up," *BusinessWeek*, April 9, 1979.

Katz, Donald, *Just Do It: The Spirit of Nike in the Corporate World* (New York: Random House, 1994).

"Track Payments," *Sports Illustrated*, March 10, 1969.

Low, Kathleen, "In the days when sports shoes weren't fashionable," *Footwear News*, October 6, 1985.

Lasch, Christopher, *The Culture of Narcissism* (New York: W.W. Norton, 1979).

MacDonald, Laurie, "Selling high tech; marketing footwear," *Footwear News*, May 20, 1996.

MacCallum, Jack, "Foot Soldiers of Fortune," *Sports Illustrated*, January 23, 1984.

Katz, Donald, "Triumph of the Swoosh," *Sports Illustrated*, August 16, 1993.

Shaquille O'Neal and Jack MacCallum, *Shaq Attack!* (New York: Hyperion, 1994).

Levine, Joshue, "Badass sells," *Forbes*, April 21, 1997.

Dyson, Michael Eric, *Reflecting Black: African American Cultural Criticism* (Minneapolis: University of Minnesota Press, 1993).

Pereira, Joseph, "Street Feat: Airs, Alphas, 'Boks and BKs are sneaking into Middle America, *The Wall Street Journal*, December 12, 1988.

Wolfe, Tom, *The Bonfire of the Vanities* (New York: Farrar, Straus and Giroux, 1987).

Telander, Rick, "Senseless," *Sports Illustrated*, May 14, 1990.

King, Stephen, "The Body," *Different Seasons* (New York: Viking, 1982).

Berger, Warren, "They Know Bo," *The New York Times*, November 11, 1990.

Jensen, Jeff, "Nike's Got Gumption," *Advertising Age*, August 1, 1994.

Elliott, Stuart, "The Spot on the Cutting-Room Floor; Reebok's Suit Over 'Jerry MaGuire' Shows Risks of Product Placement," *New York Times*, February 7, 1997.

"Big Air," *Sportstyle*, September 1996.

"Early Warning," *World Press Review*, March 1997.

Ramirez, Anthony, "The Pedestrian Sneaker Makes a Comeback," *The New York Times*, October 14, 1990.

Sloan, Pat, "Canvas shoes bound back into market," *Advertising Age*, October 24, 1988.

Chapter Two

Willigan, Geraldine E., "High Performance Marketing: An Interview with Nike's Phil Knight," *Harvard Business Review*, July/August 1992.

Herman, Valli, "Peak Performance; Athletic shoes have caught on beyond sports. Now companies can hardly keep up with demand," *The Dallas Morning News*, March 5, 1997.

James A. Ashton-Miller, Robert A. Ottaviana, Christopher Hutchinson, and Edward M. Wojtys, "What best protects the inverted weight-bearing ankle against further inversion? Evertor muscle strength compares favorably with shoe height, athletic tape, and three orthoses," *The American Journal of Sports Medicine*, November 21, 1996, No. 6, Vol. 24.

Johnson, Randy, "Domination by Design," *Metropolis*, June 1997.

Manning, Jeff, "Building a Better Shoe," *The Oregonian*, January 16, 1996.

Patton, Phil, "The Tyranny of the Swoosh," *AIGA Journal of Graphic Design* (1996).

Ricklefs, Roger, "Marketers Seek Out Today's Coolest Kids to Plug Into Tomorrow's Mall Trends," *The Wall Street Journal*, July 11, 1996.

Gladwell, Malcolm, "The Coolhunt," *The New Yorker*, March 17, 1997.

Homan, Becky, "Put on Your High-Heeled Sneakers," *St. Louis Post-Dispatch*, May 10, 1997.

Boehning, Julie C., "Keds turns to Oldham for fresh silhouette," *Footwear News*, December 2, 1996.

Feit, Josh, "The Nike Psyche," *Willamette Week*, May 28, 1997.

Leibowitz, Ed, "The Ultimate Trendoid," *Los Angeles Times*, December 8, 1996.

Smith, Geoffrey, "Reebok is tripping over its own laces," *BusinessWeek*, February 26, 1996.

Wells, Melanie, "Converse Courts Bad-Boy Image; Foot soldiers help sell street chic," *USA Today*, June 16, 1997.

"Sneaker Tale," *New York Press*, September 10, 1997.

Bannon, Timothy F., "The Birth of Pronation," *Harper's*, May 1983.

Chapter Three

Sullivan, Walter, "If the Shoe Floats, Follow It," *The New York Times*, September 22, 1992.

Converse Co., *The History of Converse, Inc. 1908-1996*.

Greider, William, *One World, Ready or Not: The Manic Logic of Global Capitalism* (New York: Simon and Schuster, 1997).

Michael T. Donaghu and Richard Barff, "Nike Just Did It: International Subcontracting and Flexibility in Athletic Footwear Production," *Regional Studies*, December 1990, Volume 24, Number 6.

Lamme, Robert, "The old soft shoe: Converse's 77-year-old basketball shoe keeps 'em jumping in Lumberton," *Business-North Carolina*, April 1994, Vol. 14; No. 3.

Allen, Mike, "Footwear company finds the shoe fits in Vista," *San Diego Business Journal*, February 26, 1996, Vol. 17; No. 9.

Richard Barff and J. Austen, "'It's gotta be da shoes': domestic manufacturing, international subcontracting, and the production of athletic footwear," *Environment and Planning A*, 1993, Vol. 25.

Ballinger, Jeff, "Nike Does it to Vietnam," *Multinational Monitor*, March 1997.

Sparrow, David, "Fragile China," *Sportstyle*, May 1996.

Fischer, David, "Global Hopscotch," *U.S. News & World Report*, June 5, 1995.

Gary N. Munthe and Alex Mirza Huzom, "Fast Track," *Indonesia Business Weekly*, February 26, 1993, Vol. 1; No. 11.

"Indonesia: labor Market Policies and International Competitiveness," Policy Research Paper 1515, *World Bank Development Report 1995*.

Ballinger, Jeff, "Nike: The New Free Trade Heel," *Harper's*, August 1992.

Chan, Anita, "Boot Camp at the Shoe Factory, Where Taiwanese Bosses Drill Chinese Workers to Make Sneakers for American Joggers," *Washington Post*, November 3, 1996.

Jeff Ballinger and Claes Olsson, eds., *Behind the Swoosh: The Struggle of Indonesians Making Nike Shoes* (Uppsala, Sweden: Global Publications Foundation, 1997).

Jeff Atkinson and Tim Connor, "Sweating for Nike: Labour conditions in the sport shoe industry," Community Aid Abroad briefing paper, November 1996.

Gde Anugrah Arka and Rin Hindryati, "Business Values Cause Labor Unrest," *Indonesia Business Weekly*, August 20, 1993, Vol. 1; No. 36.

Corn, David, "Pump up the pretense; Reebok and Human Rights," *The Nation*, August 26, 1991.

Clifford, Mark, "The China Connection: Nike is making the most of all that cheap labor," *Far Eastern Economic Review*, November 5, 1995.

Sender, Henny, "Sprinting to the Forefront; Shoemaker Yue Yuen is a Taiwanese success in China," *Far Eastern Economic Review*, August 1, 1996.

Global Exchange, "Executive Summary of Report on Nike and Reebok in China," September 1997.

Shorrock, Tim, "Vietnam protects its labor force; Foreign investors face fines for infractions," *Journal of Commerce*, July 7, 1997.

Stewart, Ian, "Unhappy Factory Workers Speaking Up in Vietnam," *Chattanooga Free Press*, June 29, 1997.

Herbert, Bob, "Mr. Young Gets it Wrong," *The New York Times*, June 27, 1997.

Glass, Stephen, "The Young and the Feckless," *The New Republic*, September 8, 1997.

Chapter Four

"If the Shoe (or Pants) Fit, Kids Will Wear Them," *Selling to Kids*, December 10, 1997.

Sanders, Lauren, "Nibbling Away at Nike; advertising for smaller athletic footwear companies," *Shoot*, January 24, 1997.

Savan, Leslie, *The Sponsored Life* (Philadelphia: Temple University Press, 1994).

Magiera, Marcy, "Nike plans rebound with fashion shoe," *Advertising Age*, January 25, 1988.

Rothenberg, Randall, *Where the Suckers Moon: The Life and Death of an Advertising Campaign* (New York: Alfred A. Knopf, 1994).

Tompkins, Richard, "'I Can' will just do it better, Nike Hopes," *The Financial Times*, January 2, 1998.

Neel Chowdhury and Anthony Paul, "Where Asia Goes From Here," *Fortune*, November 24, 1997.

Hoberman, John, *Darwin's Athletes: How Sport Has Damaged Black America and Preserved the Myth of Race* (New York: Houghton Mifflin, 1997).

Chapter Five

Tuck, Andrew, "The Hype War at Your Feet," *The Independent*, August 13, 1995.

Beatty, Sally Goll, "Sneaker politics; Bad-boy Nike plays diplomat in China," *Minneapolis Star-Tribune*, November 12, 1997.

Rawsthorn, Alice, "Trainers Take a Fashionable Leap Forward," *The Financial Times*, October 6, 1988.

McKay, Dierdre, "Price wars: athletic retailers pitch price in line with local competition," *Footwear News*, July 27, 1992.

Lagnado, Ike, "The highs and lows of women's shoe sales," *Footwear News*, April 29, 1996.

Susan Pulliam and Laura Bird, "Season's Casual Shoe Trend Means Some Firms Will Get Stomped," *The Wall Street Journal*, August 28, 1997.

Pener, Degen, "$neakers; Entertainment Companies Get Off to a Running Start in the Athletic Footwear Business," *Entertainment Weekly*, October 10, 1997.

Index

foreign competition, 14-16
hip-hop culture, 31-38
lifestyle shoe, 42-47
marketing explosion, 16-25
materials technology, 23
name of "sneaker," 9
1950's and 1960's, 12-16
1970's marketing, 16-25
1980's obsessions, 25-41
present distinctiveness, 3-8
shoe camps, 30
summary of, 172
timeline, 2-5
vintage sneakers, 46
Hi-Tec, 21
Hitler, Adolf, 11
Hoberman, John, 138
Hoffman, Dustin, 21
Hood Rubber, 4
Hoop Dreams (film), 137
Hopper, Dennis, 63

Indonesia, 84, 86, 89-94, 95,
    107-10, 111, 112
Indonesia Business Weekly,
    89, 92
In Strange Company, 9
Iverson, Allen, 32, 66, 73

Jack Purcells, 13
Jackson, Bo, 54, 127
Jackson, Jesse, 39
Jackson, Reggie, 22
Jenner, Bruce, 23, 24
Jeong, Whanil, 87
Jerry Maguire (film), 44
Jobs, Steven, 7

jogging, 16-17, 22, 23-24
Johnson, Michael, 39, 52-54
Jordan, Michael, viii, 10, 18, 24,
    28-30, 39-40, 43, 54, 97, 99,
    101, 113, 125, 172, 173
Journal of Commerce, 96
Just Do It (Katz), 18, 23, 86-88

Kaepa, 40
Kani, Kari, 40
Katz, Donald, 18, 86-88, 91, 107
Keds, x, 8, 14, 21, 22-23, 25, 40,
    46, 47, 172
    advertising and marketing, 120
    fashion shift, 69-70
    market share, xi
    Pro-Keds, 22, 28, 46
Kidd, Dusty, 108
King, Bernard, 124
King, Stephen, 40
Kinney company, 21
Knight, Philip "Buck," 27, 39,
    55, 87, 92, 107, 112, 113, 115,
    129, 131
K-Swiss, xi, 40

L.A. Gear, xi, 25, 39-40, 103, 122
Lasch, Christopher, 23
Lauren, Ralph, 32
Laver, Rod, 22
Leach, William, 173
Led Zeppelin, 21
Lee, Spike, viii, 32, 39, 127,
    144-45, 172
Lee, T.H., 87-88
Lennon, John, 24, 127
Leo, John, 41

Lichtenstein, Roy, 21
Liewald, Bob, 50-51
Lloyd, Chris Evert, 22
Loewy, Raymond, 65
Los Angeles Times, 71, 137, 138, 143
Lotto, 42
Louis-Dreyfus, Robert, 12

McEnroe, John, 132
MacMurray, Fred, 50
Mailer, Norman, 121
Malone, Karl, 122
Malone, Moses, 132
Mann, Bill, 13
manufacturing and distribution
    Asian shift, 77-78, 80
    Chinese production, 85, 86,
        93, 94-96, 100, 106-7
    fiscal crisis in Asia, 111-12
    foreign vs. domestic
        production, 76-84
    Indonesian production,
        89-94, 95,
        107-10, 112
    labor abuse issues, 91-113
    low-wage workers, 77-78,
        85-113
    South Korean production,
        84-88, 102-6
    tariff question, 79, 82-84
    Vietnamese production, 86,
        96-99, 112, 113
    women workers' movement,
        99, 100-11
Marbury, Stephon, 43
marketing. *See* advertising
    and marketing

177

**CARDS MUST REMAIN IN THIS
POCKET AT ALL TIMES**
a charge will be made for
lost or damaged cards

**BERKELEY COLLEGE
WESTCHESTER CAMPUS LIBRARY**
99 Church Street
White Plains, NY 10601